Betrayal
in
Charleston

Betrayal
in
Charleston

Extortion, Torture, and FBI Sting

Steven Sarkela
with Jack Watts

DUNHAM
books

Trade Paperback ISBN: 978-09973973-83
E-book ISBN: 978-09973973-90

Library of Congress Control Number: 201695327

Printed in the United States of America

Table of Contents

Preface

Growing up in southern Washington, nature's beauty was all around me. Having experienced nothing else, I assumed every place was equally as beautiful. Unfortunately, that isn't the case. Although I didn't appreciate it as a child, over the years its beauty has grown to have a special place in my heart.

Half a century later, I look back nostalgically and with such wonder, at numerous things about my youth—especially the magnificence of my surroundings. Hi! My name is Steve Sarkela and this is my story. Since I haven't lived in a vacuum, this has to be, by necessity, the story of several others as well.

You've heard it said that truth is stranger than fiction, haven't you? I think we all have. In my case, this is definitely true as you will soon learn. Nevertheless, to protect the innocent, I have used fictitious names throughout the book, as well as numbers in accounting.

Given the choice, I would have preferred for my story to not be as interesting as it is. If I could have controlled my destiny, which I once foolishly believed I could, I certainly would have picked a far different outcome. I would have opted to traverse a different road and go on a different journey. That wasn't an option for me—at least not completely.

Like most people, I wanted my life to count for something—for it to have profound meaning—rather than be a sermon illustrating what not to do. My fate has been far different though. Forces beyond my control have made my goal virtually impossible to achieve. That being said, if nothing else, my journey has been interesting. I'm sure you will agree with me about that—once you've read my story. It's a doozy.

Just to be clear, I'm not excusing myself from any mistakes or culpability. I'm responsible and accountable for everything that happened. Then again, so are others. If I hadn't made some poor choices along the way, I wouldn't have such a great story to tell. I like to think that thinking of my circumstances in the way one thinks of a glass being half full instead of empty, has helped me come to positive terms with how my life has been shaped and lived.

Telling my tale has required the aid of others. They have helped me bring my story to life and I want to thank them. I would like to thank my wonderful and supportive wife, Lillemor. She has been my constant source of support and my most trusted confidant. If not for her, this story and my life would not have been as meaningful and exciting. You are the most important person to me. Thank you, Lillemor.

I also want to thank my older brother, Rodney, who has always stood by my side—just like you would want and expect a brother to do. I also want to acknowledge my five children for their support. My youngest, Daniel, has helped me put these extraordinary events on paper. For his counsel in helping me overcome the issues my kidnapping and torture created, I want to add a special word of thanks to Dr. Steve Vensal. I also want to thank David Dunham, of Dunham Books, for believing in me and helping me bring this project to fruition. I also want to thank Jack Watts for his friendship and for assisting me with writing my story. To all of you, I am deeply appreciative. You are my heroes. I am indeed thankful.

—Steve Sarkela
West Palm Beach, Florida

Chapter 1

It All Starts
At the Beginning

G rowing up in Southern Washington State, I remember walking outside in the morning to look up at Mount Hood. You couldn't miss it. It dominated the skyline, especially on clear days when it wasn't raining. Unfortunately, it rained at least nine months out of the year, so there were many days when it seemed like it wasn't even there.

Nevertheless, when it was clear, there was no prettier place on earth than this place where I grew up. Since Mount Hood stands over 11,000 feet—more than two miles in elevation—it's impossible to miss—especially its snowcapped peak that glistens in the sun. It's a breathtaking and awe-inspiring sight to watch the wind blow snow flurries in rainbow colors as they catch the light. It's like a snow globe—so majestic that it's difficult to describe.

When tourists see this for the first time, they become enchanted by the view. Expecting to enjoy this sight daily, many move to the area. However, they are quickly disappointed since it rains nearly nine months of the year. Disillusionment inevitably sets in and many move away, never to return.

Our family wasn't like that. We had deep roots in the Pacific Northwest; beginning from the time my ancestors emigrated from

Finland a century earlier. They came, leaving the Baltics behind because of their religious beliefs. Southern Washington was where I was born in 1961, in Battle Ground—just north of Portland, Oregon. It's a quaint little town near the Columbia River. I spent my entire adolescence there and eventually graduated from Battleground High School in 1979.

Although my surroundings were pristine and serene, my childhood certainly wasn't. It would be nice to say that I was a really good kid growing up—never giving my parents a moment of trouble—but that would be inaccurate. I actually got into trouble quite a bit. Nothing serious, of course, but my behavior was definitely unacceptable—especially to my mother. She and I always had conflicts stemming from my innately rebellious nature.

She didn't like the way I behaved—not one bit. Fully intent on breaking my spirit, her motto was, "Spare the rod and you spoil the child." She wasn't just a firm disciplinarian—not by a long shot. It seemed like she enjoyed whipping me with a stick much more than she should have. None of my friends or siblings were punished as often or as severely as I was. At least this is how I remember it.

Sure, I was rebellious and rambunctious, but I was just a kid. When I was a little boy, if I was late, didn't do my chores or talked back to her, my mother got her stick out and beat me with it mercilessly. A half century later, I can still feel its sting on the back of my legs and my rear end. Frequently, I had raised welts, which are entirely unacceptable by today's standards. Back then, nobody thought a thing about it.

Since there were seven children in the family—that's right, seven—she obviously had her hands full. Despite being busy, she always found time to throttle me for breaking one of her many rules—even the minor ones. My dad, Harmon Sarkela, a former Marine, wasn't like her. He was firm but always fair. My mother wasn't. She was harsh, rigid and a little cruel, to be honest.

My mom, whose maiden name was Eileen Jesse Ringler, was raised in a similar fashion. That probably explains her reasons for inflicting pain. You see, we were raised in the Apostolic Lutheran Church—a very legalistic, hyper-conservative offshoot of Lutheranism. It was founded in Lapland, Finland, in the 1870's, as a campaign to counteract rampant drunkenness among Laplanders.

Railing against dissipation in general, and alcoholism specifically, a Lutheran evangelist, named Lars Levi Laestadius, preached a message of total abstinence and rigid conformity to a pietistic lifestyle. Many who witnessed the wastefulness and abuse that accompanied alcoholism responded to his message of revivalism by religiously adhering to his strict mandates of sobriety.

Some in our small sect, who longed for a fresh start, migrated to the United States. They settled primarily in semi-closed communities in New Hampshire, Minnesota and Washington. My ancestors were among those who chose to move west.

When I say our denomination was strict, I'm talking world-class legalism. For example, in the area where we lived in Southern Washington, many were involved in farming. One of the crops Apostolic Lutherans grew was strawberries. When the women from our denomination went out in the fields to harvest the produce, they were not allowed to wear jeans or shorts. This was considered to be immodest. Instead, they had to wear dresses that came down to their ankles. This certainly wasn't practical if you had to harvest fruit in a strawberry patch. To adhere to the unyielding rules of the denomination, the women wore dresses— just like they were required to do—but they also worn jeans underneath.

I'm not kidding. This is how rigid and unrelenting Apostolic Lutheranism is. Having said that, it's not surprising that my wayward, rebellious ways were met with harsh, punitive discipline—all aimed at breaking my spirit.

I understood all of this—sort of—but I didn't accept it. I didn't intend to conform either. It just wasn't in me to be the way they wanted me to be. My stubbornness matched my mom's will and more. If my never-ending discipline had been administered with love, things would've been very different. But I never felt that the manner in which she chose to deal with me came from a loving place.

I'll never forget what happened when I was ten years old. Not having obeyed one of her rules, which were voluminous, I was "switched." When I was sent to my room, I saw that my little suitcase had been packed and was lying on my bed.

Looking at my mom through my tears I asked, "Why is my suitcase packed?"

Without emotion, my mother responded, "Because I'm giving you up for adoption. That's why!"

That was all she said. Closing the door behind her as she exited, she left me to sit in my room in terrified silence. I'll never forget how I felt sitting there looking at my meager belongings and not know where I was going. Although it had been a warm day, I felt a cold chill inside. A dreadful foreboding filled my heart—I was scared. It was at that exact moment that I felt as though my mother didn't really love me.

As young as I was, this was an earth shattering and unforgettable experience for me. It let me know my suspicions were accurate. My mother, Eileen Jesse Ringler, who everybody called Jesse, but was pronounced "Jezzy," didn't love me. I had wondered whether or not she did, but now I knew for certain that she didn't. Nothing has ever changed my mind about the way I felt that day either. Obviously, this has been a very sad and painful part of my life.

Because I felt that she didn't love me, I couldn't trust her like other kids my age trusted their mothers. While I was still sitting in my room waiting to be given up for adoption, my dad came home. When he did, I heard the muffled sounds of arguing downstairs. I'm not sure what was said but I do know that by the time I was ready for bed, my suitcase had been unpacked and I was back in the family. The only thing that remained packed was my heart. Something inside of me had changed and I was never completely comfortable with my mother again.

I felt the exact opposite way about my dad. To this day, I can still remember how grateful I was that he had stood up for me—just like he always did. Being an ex-Marine, confronting injustice was something he was used to doing. This made me very proud to be his son and that has never changed.

Because it's important, let me add this: I'm telling you this story—not to make my mom look bad—not at all—but because it's an important part that will help explain future events as you will come to see.

Although I hoped things would get better for me at home, they never did. The estranged relationship between my mother and I remained. In fact, the gulf between us widened even more. From my perspective, she didn't love me or like me most of the time. Because of how she felt towards me, I never trusted her completely. It seemed like my mother had it in for me no matter what the situation happened to be.

In her eyes, I could never do anything right. So I finally stopped trying to do things the way she wanted me to do them. In the summer of my junior year at Battle Ground High School, our family made our annual trek to Minnesota to attend our denominational conclave. At this time, I began to start thinking about what my life would be like free from her. My mind turned to girls and the possibility of romance.

Not surprisingly, while the adults attended religious services, there were numerous activities planned for young people like me. Because we were expected to marry within our denomination, courtship outside of our community was strictly forbidden. Consequently, Minnesota became our spawning ground. Despite my rebellious nature, I did understand the wisdom of marrying within the faith. From the moment we arrived, my older brother, Rodney and I, never took our eyes off of the girls. It was wonderful in the sense that it was like never being able to eat sweets and then being turned loose in a candy store to pick out a special treat.

One evening, a bunch of the kids got in the back of a pickup truck to take a ride together for a scheduled youth event. There were at least ten of us in the truck, including several cute girls. As we were about to leave, my mom spotted me. Signaling for the truck to stop just as we were heading out, she bellowed, "Steve, get out of that truck. You're not going."

Looking bad in front of all of the other kids, especially the girls, this was the most mortifying moment of my life—bar none. It was truly awful and I still wince every time I think about it. Having no choice in the matter other than to obey her, I got out and watched my brother drive off with the pretty girls. I was left behind standing in the dust next to my mom, stripped of my dignity and self-worth.

With a lump in my throat and tears in my eyes I turned to my mother and yelled, "Two years!" Saying nothing else and still smarting from my public humiliation, I stomped off. She knew exactly what I meant by two years though. That was when I would graduate high school and her reign of terror in my life would end. When that day arrived, I would never again live under her thumb or be ruled by her unfair dictates. As you can imagine, I counted down the days like Christmas was coming.

Chapter 2

Finding True Love

True to my word, when I ended my formal education by graduating from Battle Ground High in 1979—a solid C student—I left home and never looked back. Being eager to make my mark in the world, I never intended to waste time going to college anyway. Academia wasn't for me. Besides, if I had gone to college, which was out of the question, it would have necessitated substantial financial help from my parents. That was something I definitely did not want. It would have kept me under my mother's thumb for another four years. There was no way I was going to allow her to continue to rule and dictate my life.

Moving out shortly after graduation, I got my own apartment and began working in the construction industry. I loved it. I was outside all day rather than being cooped up in a classroom. It also meant that I was able to work with my hands. Unlike my steady, mediocre C's, I was talented at construction. Although it often requires decades for some people to find their niche in life, if they ever do, I had found mine and I was just eighteen years old.

Being the middle child of seven, I was used to living in a house filled with people. Now on my own, the quiet and solitude made me uncomfortable—especially in the evenings and on the weekends. I didn't find much joy in carousing, either. I did it a little, but it never set well with me.

I guess being an Apostolic Lutheran was something that had settled in my bones. Perhaps I wasn't quite as rebellious as some people thought? Besides, dissipation left an emotional hangover I just couldn't get past. It made me feel bad about myself. Unlike so many of my friends in construction, it was a lifestyle I just couldn't embrace. So, with all the wisdom an eighteen-year-old can possess, I made a life-altering decision. I resolved to take a wife—not a lover, a wife.

Loyola once said, "Give me a child until he is seven and I will give you a Catholic for life." Although I was Apostolic Lutheran and not Catholic, Loyola's point still rang true. My mindset was thoroughly Apostolic Lutheran. For better or worse, despite my deep-seated rebellious nature, my thinking process conformed to my denomination's viewpoint. It meant I couldn't just date, have a girl friend and enjoy fornication like everybody else was doing in 1980. Although I tried to live like this, I couldn't handle the guilt it produced. With my hormones raging—like every other guy my age—and being a man of the world, I set out to get married. Not just any pretty woman would do though—no way.

The next time our denominational conclave met in Minnesota, my agenda was firmly set. I intended to find a wife. My prospective bride had to be someone within our small denomination—someone chosen by the Lord. Nobody less would be acceptable. Intuitively, I understood this. How could I ever forget it? It had been drummed into my brain from the time I was old enough to attend Sunday school.

Perhaps this sounds a little unusual to you, maybe even a little weird, but it wasn't to me. There are many other religious groups who practice the same thing. Jewish people certainly marry among themselves. So do the Amish and many Roman Catholics for that matter. They marry within their communities—just like we did. For me to behave differently was out of the question. I never even considered it despite being told regularly how rebellious I was.

Thus, my agenda was set. I didn't announce it to anyone—not even my older brother, Rodney. Arriving at the church convention for a weeklong stay, I spotted my future wife almost immediately. She didn't know it, but I certainly did. I knew it the moment I saw her.

Not having seen her for a couple of years, I was amazed at how beautiful she had become. No longer a little girl, I was smitten the moment I saw her. Making an impulsive, life-altering decision, I knew that Hester Dimesdale was the girl for me. I wanted to marry her and no one else. There was no doubt in my mind—no hesitation at all! But there was a big problem—she was only sixteen years old. Even in our denomination where couples marry early, Hester was considered to be very young. I suppose being eighteen at the time made me pretty young too.

Despite her age, I never deviated from my decision to make her my bride—not one iota. More than a third of a century later, I can still remember how beautiful she looked that day I saw her back in 1980—the year Ronald Reagan beat Jimmy Carter and became our 38th president.

It wasn't just that Hester Dimesdale was pretty. It was more than that. She had a wholesome quality about her that made me feel empowered and purposeful just being around her. I felt like I was in the presence of a godly woman, my soul mate—a woman who would love and honor me for the rest of our lives. Unlike my mother, I was certain Hester would never betray me. How could she? She didn't have a devious or deceitful bone in her body.

When she smiled at me, which she did frequently, often even winking when she did, my heart would leap with love and yearning. I couldn't help myself. I was completely enchanted by her. I loved her smile. Not only was it warm, engaging and winsome, it also revealed her beautiful teeth. Just having had her braces removed, her teeth were perfectly straight, which was a rarity in those days.

Standing 5' 5" tall, like everything else about her, her posture was perfect and made her seem almost regal. Her movements were so elegant and graceful. Nothing about her betrayed how young she was. On the contrary, she carried herself like a woman and not like a girl, which made her even more appealing. Just watching the way she moved stirred me. I couldn't help myself. Having a trim athletic figure, Hester looked like she could have been an Olympic athlete. This didn't mean she was overly muscular because she wasn't.

Her best feature by far was her thick brown hair, which she teased and wore shoulder length—just like Farrah Fawcett did on *Charlie's Angels*, my favorite show. Hester's hair accented her sparkling blue eyes, which were just a hair off center. Instead of spoiling her beauty, it actually enhanced it—at least in my eyes. She was so beautiful and charming that everyone was captivated by her too.

Since our denominational convention campground in Minnesota was widely known as the spawning ground for Apostolic Lutherans, I wasn't the only one who recognized Hester's charm and beauty. Others did too. That summer she had numerous suitors hovering around her, but I didn't care. Once I fixated my focus on her, having just one goal in mind, I pursued her vigorously and relentlessly. What I think Hester liked about me the most was how I carried myself so confidently. The fact that I never hesitated or second-guessed myself must have been very appealing to her. But that wasn't her only motivation to be interested in me. Hester had troubles of her own at home. She had sixteen siblings, which made my family seem small by comparison. Being raised in New Hampshire and being tired of living at home, Hester's goals were similar to mine. She wanted to get out and be on her own. So, when I made advances toward her, she responded eagerly, wholeheartedly and without reservation. I was as acceptable to her as she was to me. Our worlds were in alignment.

Early one evening, instead of attending a function that was scheduled for young people like us, we skipped it and decided to spend some time together—alone. Once we reached our secluded spot and knew we would not be disturbed, I reached over and kissed her for the first time. It was magical.

There was no hesitation on her part. She responded as enthusiastically as I did—just like I had hoped she would. Within a few seconds, we were lost in each other's embrace. Our connection was quick, spontaneous and effortless, but we didn't go all the way. We came close—like millions of other kids our age would have—but we stopped just short of consummating our love, knowing that our union was reserved for the marital bed.

By the time the conference was over and I headed west and she headed east, we both knew that we wanted to spend the rest of our lives together. That week in Minnesota had been enchanting—just like it had been scripted for a movie. We were in love with each other. That's the good news, but there was also some bad news. By the time I reached Washington and returned to work, I was miserable. Completely distracted, I did my work, but my heart was no longer in construction. It was with her. All I could think about was Hester Dimesdale and how much I wanted to be with her. The passion she had aroused in me needed sating and I had no intention of waiting for a year or two until we both got a little older to make her my wife.

With all the spontaneity, impulsivity and foolhardiness of youth, I called her and asked her to marry me. Because she was just as miserable without me as I had been without her, when I brought up the subject of marriage she was equally enthusiastic. When I popped the question, she responded with an affirmative, "Yes, Steve, I'll marry you."

I felt certain she would agree. If I hadn't, I wouldn't have asked. I will admit that when she accepted my proposal and said yes, it was so empowering. I felt like Superman and as if I could leap a tall building in a single bound. My life was about to change. I was about to be fulfilled. I was going to have exactly what I wanted and I would never be lonely again. I was certain of it.

Even better, my raging hormones would be sated in the way God would honor. He was about to bless me with a beautiful bride—a woman who would love me, share my life and my bed.

Chapter 3

She Always Gets What She Wants

ndeed, I was a lucky man. But we had a big problem—her age. Being sixteen, she couldn't get married without her parent's permission. She wasn't old enough, according to the state laws of New Hampshire. Like most states, New Hampshire considered Hester to be too young to make such life-altering decisions without the consent of her parents. Nevertheless, we were determined to move forward with our plans.

When Hester told her mother, Eunice, what she intended to do, Mrs. Dimesdale balked at the idea as Hester predicted she would.

"You are not nearly mature enough to get married, Hester," Mrs. Dimesdale scolded. Angrily, she added, "I will not give you my permission—never in a million years. That settles it. You are not getting married until you are at least eighteen."

Hester pleaded her case by telling her mother how much she loved me. However, Mrs. Dimesdale would not change her mind. Ending the conversation, Mrs. Dimesdale said, "The answer is no and it's not going to change."

Softening a moment later and placing her arms around Hester, who had started crying, Mrs. Dimesdale raised her daughter's face and looked into her eyes. In a tender, almost pleading voice, Eunice added, "Hester, I love you. You know that, don't you? You're just beginning your junior year of high school. Why would you want to throw your life away by marrying when you are so young?"

Hester really didn't have a good answer at the time. She certainly didn't want to tell her mom it was because she was sick of living at home. Hester never even intimated how badly she wanted to get out of the house. So, she wisely said nothing and continued to cry on her mother's shoulder for a while, allowing her mom to comfort her in her disappointment.

Realizing she was unlikely to make any further progress with her mother, Hester, who was used to getting her way, especially with her father, changed her strategy. Abandoning her efforts to enlist her mother's support, which she realized would be futile, Hester decided to approach her father instead.

Hester's dad, Ahab Dimesdale, a tall, handsome and respected leader in our denomination, had a soft spot in his heart for his daughter. Lots of fathers, even powerful leaders like Ahab, have a difficult time saying no to their children.

Everybody in the Apostolic Lutheran community knew who he was and most considered him to be wise. Like E.F. Hutton, whenever Ahab spoke, people listened. He was very important within our community, but was influential even beyond our religious group.

A gifted speaker and Bible teacher, Ahab's counsel was widely sought by many—both in business and in spiritual matters. Being a very successful businessman, Ahab wore many hats in our small, tight, yet geographically diverse community. Congregants loved the way he elucidated God's Word by teaching it in powerful, practical and easy ways that we could understand and follow.

Nearly everyone was impressed by Ahab Dimesdale's affluence. Numerous congregants wanted to follow in his footsteps. They desired the same measure of success that the Dimesdales enjoyed.

Even though Ahab was the father of seventeen children—all by the same woman—he provided well for his family. He was so successful they even had a second home in Florida. Not to mention that all of his children were always fashionably dressed.

Growing up, Hester never wanted for much. It was something she couldn't even conceptualize. As affluent as their family was, Hester took being wealthy for granted. She was used to getting whatever she wanted, when she wanted it. Now that she intended to marry me, her focus was so intense she wouldn't take "no" for an answer.

One evening after dinner, several days after getting nowhere with her mother, Hester sat down with her parents and explained to them in detail what she intended to do. Essentially, she gave them a sales pitch on the idea of marrying me. She confidently asserted that it was God's will that she marry me and the two of them should aid her in fulfilling God's will for her by agreeing to let her marry. She was sure they didn't want to stand in the way of Providence. The impact of her plea and reasoning could be seen on her father's face.

Hester's mother remained adamantly opposed to the idea. However, her dad, who had difficulty saying no to his strong willed daughter, had begun to warm up to the idea. Hester could tell the tide was turning in her favor and so she continued to press harder.

For her, getting her own way was at least as important as achieving her goal. Winning was everything to Hester. Sighing, Ahab finally relented. He looked at his wife and said, "She seems to know what she's doing Eunice, and her love for Steve Sarkela seems genuine. I think it will work out just fine. I really do."

Startled by her husband's capitulation, all Eunice could do was stare at Ahab blankly, absolutely dumbfounded by the foolishness of what she was hearing.

Oblivious to the depth of his wife's opposition—just like he was to most of Eunice's feelings—Ahab concluded, "At least

Steve's in the denomination. If she wants to get married Eunice, I'll sign the papers and give her the go-ahead."

With this enunciation, which effectively settled the matter in Hester's favor, her mother—although unwilling to challenge her husband's authority—remained dead set against it. Eunice, knowing her daughter better than anyone, including her husband, was certain the plan was ill-conceived. Eunice was convinced it would end in disaster. But there was nothing she could do to change the course of events. Since further discussion was out of the question after her husband had pronounced his decision, she did the only acceptable thing she could. She burst into tears.

Trying to console her or perhaps just to look good, Ahab put his hand on her shoulder and rubbed it gently. Tenderly, he added, "Think of it this way Eunice, with Hester gone, there will be one less mouth to feed around here."

An hour later, Hester, victorious and filled with enthusiasm at having accomplished her goal, called me to announce the great news. Answering immediately on the first ring and knowing what her agenda had been, I didn't say a word. I didn't have to. She knew how eagerly I was anticipating her call.

Without pleasantries, Hester, in a playful voice simply said, "It is all set. In two months, we'll be married."

There are no words to describe how euphoric I felt after Hester's call announcing the good news. I was ecstatic. Once Hester and I disconnected, after I had time to assimilate what was about to happen, I paused to reflect and give thanks. In His wisdom and sovereignty, God had provided me with a godly woman—one within our denomination. Beautiful, smart and talented. I felt certain we would be good together and become one of the leading families in the Apostolic Lutheran denomination.

Although Hester had been quite confident she could coax her father into signing the papers, I didn't share her enthusiasm. In fact, I felt quite the opposite and had started to worry myself sick about our future. I knew how badly I wanted to marry her but also realized that we really were quite young. I was still eighteen and she was just sixteen. By any standard, other than some of those living in the Ozarks or Appalachia, we were too young to get married, have children and take care of each other.

As I reflect back on that time as a grown man in his fifties, with three daughters, I can't imagine giving any of my children permission for something as foolhardy as what we were proposing. Nevertheless, Ahab had done just that. He even gave us his blessing, which both of us greatly desired.

With the papers signed, the wedding was on.

Although we were young, we were in-love. Plus, we were committed to the same values. We shared the same desires and purpose for our life together. Our future couldn't be better positioned for success. What was to stop us? Confident of this, with my beautiful bride beside me, I intended to march boldly into the future, filled with all the wisdom an eighteen-year-old can possess.

About an hour after hearing the news from Hester, I called my parents and informed them of our plans. My mother Jezzy, in typical fashion was nonplussed. But my dad wasn't nearly as pleased as I thought he would be. Although he didn't say he wasn't too happy about our decision to marry—at least not at the time—he had some serious misgivings about me getting involved with the Dimesdale family.

At the time, my enthusiasm about marrying Hester was so intense I didn't pay attention to his misgivings. I didn't forget them either. They lingered, just below the surface in my subconscious, ready to surface some time in the future.

Two months later, my entire family traveled cross-country to New Hampshire to attend our wedding. If I were a girl, which

I obviously am not, I would take great pains to tell you about the flowers and how beautiful they were. I would also mention the fifty candles that cast a warm glow in the church, making our special occasion an affair to remember. Although the music was spectacular and the singing out of this world, bringing tears to the eyes of nearly every person present, the only thing that interested me was exchanging vows and saying our *I do's.*

Like most people, I enjoyed the reception a lot. Being cheered and affirmed by everybody, other than Hester's mother, I felt the most validated I had ever been. Even my mom seemed to have a good time. She was more gregarious and engaging than I had ever seen her, which made me feel good. Her focus wasn't just on her new daughter-in-law though. Jezzy talked at length to my new father-in-law, Ahab. This assured me that our families were developing a deep and powerful bond—one that would be beneficial to Hester and I as we made our way through life.

Not surprisingly, Hester's mom wasn't nearly as enthusiastic as her husband. Mrs. Dimesdale smiled and did her best to be pleasant, but it seemed hollow and disingenuous. This bothered me, but it certainly didn't bother my bride. In fact, I think she enjoyed it. I had a sneaking suspicion that Hester desired to make her mother very uncomfortable because she had wanted to leave home as badly as I had wanted to leave home too. Seeing her mother in so much discomfort seemed to make her wedding day even more enjoyable.

My dad, who was always somewhat reserved and a man of few words, was particularly taciturn at the wedding. Toward the end of the reception, when I shook his hand and hugged him just before Hester and I left to consummate our union, he stopped me from walking off. He did this by placing both of his strong hands on my shoulders.

Looking me straight in the eye, he said, "Steve, be careful with your new father-in-law. I know he's very successful and carries himself well, but there are a lot of rumors about his unethical deals circulating in the denomination. He's hurt some people pretty badly and he hasn't paid some folks either. If I were you, I'd be very careful around him."

I nodded my head like I understood what he had just said, but I didn't. Rather than ask him to explain what he meant, I started to walk off, paying little heed to his warning.

Realizing he had not connected, my dad squeezed my shoulders until he had my complete attention—just like he had done numerous times in my life. "Steve," he said, "I mean it. Be very careful before getting involved in any of Ahab's deals. He'll chew you up, spit you out and never think a thing about what it has done—even if it hurts Hester."

Having said that, he finally had my attention. I nodded that I heard him and understood, but I really didn't—not then anyway. At eighteen and a novice in the ways of the world, how could I? Like any other guy who had just been married, all I could think about was finally being alone with Hester.

Chapter 4

An Unhappy Wife
Makes for
An Unhappy Life

W e were married in 1980, just a few days before the Pittsburg Steelers beat the Los Angeles Rams in Super Bowl VIV and just two months after fifty-two American hostages were taken prisoner by the Islamic Revolutionaries of Ayatollah Khomeini in Iran. While the eyes of the entire world were on the Middle East, Hester and I were making sparks of our own in the coldest place in North America.

Blissfully unconcerned about what was going on in the world, getting married had been our sole priority. We didn't even care how cold it was in Northern New England in January. Our only alternative to getting married in the snowy mountains would have been to wait until it began to warm up in the spring.

After our short honeymoon, which was the first time we were able to spend quality time together and really get to know one another, my new bride returned with me to the Pacific Northwest. It was the first time she had ever been there and agreed that it was as beautiful as I said it was.

Once home in Southern Washington, we began living life as a normal married couple. Because I worked in construction, I left early in the morning before she got out of bed. The long and hard workdays didn't matter. I was just happy to have her there beside me. I always kissed her forehead tenderly before heading off to work and made sure it was the last thing I did before leaving.

For a short while, we led an ideal life like most newlyweds. But it didn't last long. Adjusting to married life can be difficult. It takes maturity to work through problems. And being just eighteen and sixteen, respectively, neither of us had many real life experiences. Working through difficult situations also takes willingness and perseverance, which I had, but she didn't.

Hester, being the daughter of a prosperous businessman, was used to living an affluent life. She was accustomed to having what she wanted when she wanted it, regardless of what it was, especially items to aid her "beautification." She was also used to buying new clothes and fine jewelry, which were things we couldn't afford.

To say the concept of delayed gratification was foreign to Hester would be a massive understatement. Although her mother had the ability to say no to Hester and make it stick—her father never could. Consequently, my bride was used to getting her way about everything and had no intention of changing her ways. This was especially true when it came to spending money. Doing without was something she had never done—and wouldn't even try to understand.

When I came home on Friday afternoons with my meager paycheck in hand, Hester was less than pleased. Not having any experience at budgeting or being frugal, Hester had no interest in learning how to make ends meet. At first, she was just cross with me for not making more than I did, but then her antipathy with being financially constrained escalated. Eventually, she became quite rebellious. Scarcity and want produced discord between us. This led to acrimony, which eventually culminated in fighting. Soon, our blissful apartment turned into a war zone.

On our best days, we bickered quite a bit. On our worst, we screamed at each other and it was always about her not having enough money to spend. The discord between us became unbearable, but there was very little I could do to alter the situation. Still a teenager and having just graduated high school, I was making as much money as I was capable of making. Nevertheless, what I brought home wasn't enough for Hester— not nearly enough. She always wanted more.

Unfortunately, my inability to meet the financial needs required by my wife's entitled lifestyle wasn't our only issue. There was another. Adding significantly to the tension that existed between us, after just six months of marriage, Hester became pregnant. We hadn't anticipated or planned for this, but obviously we hadn't taken adequate means to prevent it, either. Since she was one of seventeen children and I was one of seven, we certainly came from a fertile lot. Although this never occurred to us at the time, it certainly should have.

So, in addition to being broke, we were also about to add a significant financial expense to our meager budget. Despite the new financial constraint and arguments that ensued because of it, I loved that Hester was pregnant because I always wanted to be a father.

Naively, I thought that having a child would bring us closer together. In a sense, it was exactly what we needed to rekindle our love. I was overjoyed! Having a baby was exactly what I wanted.

Unfortunately, it wasn't what Hester wanted. In her eyes, it tied her to me irreversibly, solidifying a bond she no longer desired. I welcomed what was happening; she didn't. In fact, her resentment grew faster than the child in her, making our home unbearable. One day, it boiled over for both of us.

With resentment in her eyes, accompanied by a mocking voice, she turned to me and scolded, "Steve, you are such a loser. You can't support me and you can't support our baby either."

"I'm doing the best I can," I said defensively, "and it will get better. I promise."

Practically sneering, she mocked me. "I should have married your brother and not you."

Her contemptuous remarks were piercing and her disrespect wounded me to the core. Even my mother had never even been this cruel and heartless. I was hurt—there was no doubt about it. Hester's words were so unexpected—especially the statement involving my older brother. Once she said it—once it was out there—she was pleased. I could see it in her eyes, but she could also see the pain on my face. It hurt me as much as it made her smile, but it certainly wasn't a smile of endearment. It was a malevolent and scornful smirk.

Even worse, I couldn't think of anything to say in response to her hateful spiel. I was furious and my anger spilled over into inappropriate action. Raising my hand, I slapped her across the face. For a second or two, I was glad I hit her. Soon after, I realized I had crossed a line and did something I could never take back. Startled, she looked at me with cold, defiant eyes. Then she turned her back and walked off, stripping me of what little was left of my dignity.

Standing there alone, I began to cry. I couldn't help it. As the reality of what I had done dawned on me, I never felt as low as I did that evening. Regardless of what she said to me or how provocative she had been, I shouldn't have slapped her. That was wrong of me and I knew it. I regretted it before she left the room, but there was nothing I could do to change my actions. I couldn't take it back.

Although I hadn't closed my fist or anything like that, I still hit her. I had violated a boundary no man should ever break, regardless of how frustrating the situation becomes. Within a few seconds, I felt horrible about what I had done, but that was just the beginning. As the days and weeks passed, my self-loathing intensified and I became depressed. The days following this encounter were dark for me. I wanted to forget what happened and sweep it under the rug, but I couldn't. It happened. I was ashamed of myself and knew I had to take full responsibility for what I did.

It's very hard for me to admit being as wrong as I was, especially to write about it, but it's true. This is exactly what happened and how it occurred. Since I'm committed to telling you the truth, I must be forthright about everything, including my behavior and the things that cast me in a bad light.

When I married Hester, I had made a commitment to be an adult. I promised her—in front of God, family and many witnesses on that snowy day in New Hampshire—that I was mature enough to "man up" to every situation. When the going got tough though, really tough, I did the exact opposite. I behaved like a little boy and slapped the woman I had promised to love, honor and cherish. My despair over what I had done became overwhelming and practically incapacitating.

For her part, Hester had experienced enough of me. Perhaps she said what she did to provoke such a response from me in order to justify her leaving me. I'll never know for sure. What I do know is she was unwilling to stay after being slapped. She just wanted out. The next day, after having called her father to tell him what I had done, he sent her a plane ticket to come home. Without so much as a by your leave, Hester packed her bags and left without even saying goodbye. She left while I was at work, taking a Delta flight from Portland headed southeast to her parent's winter home in West Palm Beach, Florida.

When I came home that evening, the apartment was empty and so was my heart. I was alone again with nothing to fill my time other than dwelling on the pain I was feeling. My wife, who I still loved deeply, was over 3,000 miles away. What made it worse was the fact that our child, my child, was far away from me too.

Chapter 5

The Joy of Life
and The Pain of Loss

W ith Hester gone I was the most discouraged I have ever felt. She had made it clear that she had no intention of ever coming back to me. Having brought the misery on myself, I bathed in self-condemnation daily. Unable to eat, I lost weight, which I certainly didn't need. I was in a very dark place and I was afraid I would never recover from her departure.

Knowing I couldn't continue to live like this, I finally came to terms with what I needed to do. Deciding that my life had no meaning without Hester, I knew that I needed to win her back. Nothing less than making my best effort to do so would suffice. So, taking the bull by the horns, I booked a Delta flight and headed for West Palm Beach to speak to my wife in person. With no well thought out plan or, more accurately, no plan at all, I simply arrived at my in-laws' house and asked to speak to Hester. Surprised to see me, my heart broke when I saw my wife. I couldn't help myself. I started to cry, but seeing me penitent didn't move her to either compassion or forgiveness. In fact, it seemed to have the exact opposite effect.

If anything, I detected substantial contempt coming from her, mixed with residual anger, perhaps even loathing. She was still furious with me, no doubt about it. Our time apart had not mellowed her at all. Nevertheless, as each day passed, the baby inside of her continued to grow. As much as she resented me, there was nothing she could do to change the fact that it was mine. There was no question about that. Being a mother at seventeen is difficult enough, but doing so without the help and support of her child's father multiplied Hester's dilemma. Even though she hated me, she needed me—and she knew it.

Although she felt certain she had made a mistake marrying me in the first place, the baby meant she couldn't just wash her hands of me and say, "Good riddance." If she hadn't been pregnant, I feel certain that was exactly what she would've done. But, as she got bigger by the day, so did her problem. She certainly didn't want to raise our child as a single parent. Especially not as a seventeen-year-old single mother. What girl in her right mind would?

Thus, her situation, rather than her love for me, forced Hester to consider reconciliation as a viable option. Other forces were also at work, benefitting me in ways I didn't know at the time. Although Hester had been very candid with her parents about what married life had been like with me, her father, Ahab, also knew how entitled and spoiled his daughter really was. Having had to deal with her much longer than I had, he understood her entitled mentality better than I did.

Being in a "family way," Ahab wasn't about to assume the responsibility for raising his grandchild—not being the father of seventeen already. From his perspective, Ahab had done his share of child rearing and then some, despite the fact it was his wife, Eunice, who had done the lion's share of the work. Nevertheless, having the responsibility of being the breadwinner of such a large family, Ahab didn't want the responsibility for funding the following generation as well. Who could blame him—especially with me begging for the opportunity to take care of my own child? If nothing else, Ahab knew how expensive it would be. He also understood the cost required to maintain Hester in the lifestyle she required—of that he had a very clear understanding.

Because of these factors, Ahab encouraged Hester to reconcile with me by reminding her it was God's will. Consequently, shortly before our first child, Derek, was born, Hester relented and came back to me. More than anything, I was relieved she had returned, but I couldn't bask in my victory for long. Soon after her return, her water broke and she went into labor.

I was present for all of it. Fearing I would be prevented from witnessing this event, being reconciled made it that much more meaningful for me. When I first laid eyes on my son I loved him instantly. So did his mother—I could see it in her eyes. He was beautiful and looked exactly like the Gerber baby—at least I thought so. He was born March 1, 1981, fourteen months after Hester and I exchanged our wedding vows on that cold day in January. The New England wind was whirling, making it nearly impossible to be outside. Just seventeen when she became pregnant, Hester was a mother at eighteen. Not yet twenty, I had the responsibility for supporting a family of three people, which might seem overwhelming to most but, in my heart, I knew I was up to the task. While most kids our age were planning how to spend the weekend, by necessity, our thoughts were more far-reaching and certainly more serious. With a new child, we had no choice but to be mature adults and loving parents.

We couldn't have been more pleased with our infant son. If nothing else, having a family kept us together as I hoped it always would. To get her to reconcile with me late in her third trimester, I had to do some serious groveling. In fact, from then on in our marriage, groveling was required quite often—most of it unjustified. I promised her I would be an ideal husband, which I did my best to become.

Nevertheless, something between us had changed. The power position no longer resided with me. It belonged to her, and once she gained it, she refused to relinquish it—not for any reason or for any period of time.

All I wanted was for her to stay and for us to be a loving family, but it seemed like she always had one foot outside the door. Knowing how much I needed her and feared losing her, she used my insecurity to manipulate me into doing whatever she desired. This wasn't something she did every now and then. It became the dominant feature of our marriage. The threat of leaving hovered over my head constantly, relentlessly chipping away at my self-esteem, self-respect and self-confidence. Her contempt for me added significantly to my feelings of insecurity.

Within a short period of time, the self-willed rebellious kid I had always been ceased to exist. He was replaced by a man who definitely loved his wife, but the love we shared was unhealthy. I became clingy and dependent, which I hated about myself. Fear of losing Hester motivated everything I did. It became the motivating factor in all the decisions I made, triggering every thought and action I had. Although I hated myself for being this way, I lacked the intestinal fortitude to do something about it.

Whenever we argued, which was frequently—or I showed the least bit of gumption—Hester mounted an offensive to put me back in my place. She was always successful. She walked out several other times in the years that followed, but always returned. Despite all of the chaos and discord, our lives went on like this for many years. As significant as the discord was between us, you might be surprised that we had five children together. We loved each one of them just as much as we loved our first.

———◇———

There were other significant family issues in our marriage that are pertinent to telling this story and need to be divulged. Some of them are quite unusual, but they provide context and make it compelling.

As you know by now, my mother had been very hard on me growing up, which meant she had never been heroic to me. My dad on the other hand, was my hero and my champion. He was a man's man in every sense of the word. I loved my father, Harmon. I honored him and wanted to be exactly like him. Physically strong and formidable, my dad exuded a presence that everybody could see and feel. He had not just been a Marine by vocation; he was a Marine by nature and temperament. He didn't need to insist on being respected by others; he garnered their respect naturally. He was a powerful alpha male by nature and I couldn't have admired him more if I had tried. He was a man of steel—indestructible. Or so it seemed.

Despite seeming so formidable, shortly after Hester and I were married, he was diagnosed with cirrhosis of the liver. They told us it was a genetic problem and not behavioral. Maybe it was, but he was very young to have cirrhosis—just forty-two. For our entire family, especially my mother, who loved Harmon dearly, the news was devastating and difficult to bear. In the back of my mind, I've always wondered if it had anything to do with one of his "special assignments" in the Corps. This occurred to me only because the Veterans Administration was heavily involved with my dad's diagnosis.

One night, in the early 1950's, his platoon was alerted at 2 a.m and made to get ready for a mission. At the time, he was stationed in New Mexico. He and his buddies were taken deep into the desert. Once they arrived at their destination, which was in the middle of nowhere, they disembarked from their trucks and were forced to stand at attention for hours. They were not told why they were there.

Finally, at dawn, a nuclear bomb was detonated a few miles from where they were standing. The purpose for their presence was to help the Department of Defense determine what the effects of a nuclear explosion would have on them. Shockingly, they were less than five miles away from ground zero.

It wasn't as if any of them had a choice in the matter. Their presence was required. Standing there was an order and Marines always obey orders. Afterwards, a medical team examined them, pronouncing each one to be fit as a fiddle. When my dad became quite ill from a disease few non-drinkers have, I put two-and-two together in my mind. My dad, being a stalwart in the Apostolic Lutheran Denomination, was a teetotaler, which made a diagnosis of cirrhosis particularly surprising.

During this same period—the winter of 1982—my brother, Rodney, fell in-love with a young lady from our denomination. Soon afterwards, they decided to get married. Since his fiance lived in Florida, Hester, the baby and I made the trip from our home in Washington to attend the wedding. Following the ceremony, we planned to stay with Hester's mom and dad for a while. For us, it would be our first real family vacation.

The wedding, which was a sumptuous affair, was held on a Saturday afternoon. I was part of the wedding party and even Hester thought I looked quite dashing in my tuxedo, telling me so with a wink I hadn't seen for quite some time.

The wedding was truly a magnificent occasion and I was glad we made the decision to attend. Less than ten minutes after Rodney and his bride said their vows, we were called to the phone for an urgent message. The call originated from the hospital where our father was being treated for cirrhosis. The news wasn't good. He was dying and we were called back to Washington to say our goodbyes.

It was a terrible way to end a day that had started out so well. I'll never forget the long plane ride back to Washington the following morning. It was awful. Just twenty years old and I was already having to say goodbye to my father—my hero. In some ways, it must have been even harder for Rodney. Forced to postpone his honeymoon, he had the unenviable lot of having his wedding anniversary coincide with our father's death. I imagine that the sadness of our father's death will always supersede the joy of remembering the happiest day of his life. I hated this for Rodney.

When our cab pulled up to the hospital, we raced in. We made it just in time to say goodbye. We witnessed our dad's last breath on Tuesday, March 22, 1982. It's a day I will never forget. Looking at him on his deathbed, he was a shell of the man I had known my entire life. He died much too young and I have missed him terribly over the years. It's true that the good die young. His death, it seemed to me, was not due to a genetic problem.

Nothing will convince me of that.

Chapter 6

Parental In-Laws

he death of my father was difficult on all of us, but especially traumatic for my mother. It happened so quickly. One day, Dad was vibrant and full of life. The next day, he became sick, deteriorated quickly and died shortly thereafter. At least, that's the way it seemed to me. We certainly didn't expect him to die right after Rodney got married, but he did. The suddenness of it made our loss more difficult to bear.

Despite being the mother of seven, with several children still remaining at home, Jezzy was still in her early forties and was much too young to be a widow. Although I never believed she loved me, based on the way she treated me while I was growing up, I had no doubt she loved my father. We all did. He was a wonderful man and a great dad.

Decades later, I still think about him nearly every day. I think of him especially when I need godly wisdom, which is something he exuded in abundance. I depended on him a great deal, even after Hester and I got married; so did my mother. He was not only her husband, but he was also her best friend.

Unable to cope with life as a single woman, my mother, who was very attractive, began dating. She became involved with a man from our church not long after my father's passing. At first, this surprised me and I didn't like it. None of my siblings did either. It made me feel uncomfortable, but my wife helped me understand that although my father had died, my mother hadn't and she needed to go on with her life.

As my mom became more serious about her new beau, we received some very disturbing news from New Hampshire. Hester's mother, who was in her late forties, was diagnosed with breast cancer. Even worse, by the time she learned how serious her problem was, it had metastasized and spread to her lymph nodes.

Soon thereafter, Hester informed me that my mother-in-law was dying. Nothing could be done to stop the spread of the cancer. The news obviously devastated my wife. Having had to do the same thing a short while earlier, I was able to comfort her. For a short while, our mutual grief brought us closer together.

Mrs. Dimesdale fought a brave but short battle against the dreaded disease. She died shortly after being diagnosed. The news crushed my wife. Especially since there were so many unresolved conflicts between Hester and her mother that would never be addressed or resolved. The loss, however, was much worse for her father. Without his wife, Ahab was completely lost. He was unable to operate at full capacity without her. Some men simply can't function normally without a woman by their side. Ahab was one of them. Without his wife, despite being a man of wealth and influence, Ahab was unable to be the dominant force he had always been.

While all of this was transpiring in New Hampshire, back in Oregon—the other side of the continent—Jezzy's relationship with her new beau was becoming more serious by the day. My siblings and I felt certain that she would marry the man she had been dating for the past six months.

While trying to console her father, Hester mentioned Jezzy's new love interest. She intimated to Ahab that she anticipated having a new father-in-law very soon. When Ahab heard that Jezzy might remarry soon, he made a life altering, impulsive decision—even though his wife had been dead less than a month.

The next day, he went to a local jeweler in Manchester, New Hampshire and bought an expensive engagement ring—one any woman would love to own. Writing a note to accompany it, which was a marriage proposal, he sent the ring in an overnight package to his intended bride.

The following morning, my mother received the ring and the note. Obviously surprised, Jezzy was also flattered. Ahab was asking her to marry him. She tried the ring on and liked the way it looked. She also liked that Ahab was interested in her despite the fact that she was nearly engaged to another man. After speaking with him on the phone shortly thereafter, Ahab booked a flight to Portland for the following weekend.

Jezzy met Ahab at the airport sporting the ring he had given her. When Ahab saw this, although he had expressly forbidden her from wearing it before he arrived, he smiled nonetheless. After talking for a long while, Ahab made a formal proposal and Jezzy accepted.

Although she had been interested in the other man, he was not nearly as good a catch as Ahab and she knew it. Dismissing her former beau soon thereafter, Jezzy never gave the poor man another thought. She was headed in an entirely new direction—one that placed her side by side with my father-in-law, Ahab.

Within two months, they were married. Although his first wife had been dead less than six months—not yet cold in the grave—Ahab was now the happiest man on earth without her. The reason for this was obvious. He was married to my mother. Everything happened so fast, like a whirlwind, that it was difficult for us to assimilate what had happened, let alone accept it.

Ahab had a new bride, Jezzy Dimesdale. Between the two of them, they were the parents of twenty-five children, with several still at home. That's quite a sizable family. The adjustment was somewhat difficult for several of the children, but it was particularly difficult for my wife and me. It was also confusing. By marrying my mother, Ahab became my stepfather, while at the same time continuing to be my father-in-law. Adjusting to this dual role wasn't only difficult, it was also perplexing. It was even worse for my wife.

My mother, Jezzy, who had been Hester's mother-in-law, was now her stepmother as well. Because this happened less than three months after her mother's death, my wife didn't even have time to grieve her loss before being forced to accept a new woman as her stepmother. That someone other than her mother was sharing her father's bed was particularly galling to Hester. Perhaps, and this is my opinion, because she had never resolved her issues with her dead mother, Hester's antipathy about this was greater than anybody else's.

As mother-in-law and daughter-in-law, Jezzy and Hester got along well—at least as well as in-laws in a troubled marriage ever do. Our marriage was clearly problematic. Jezzy, being Hester's mother-in-law was one thing, but to also have her become her stepmother was an emotional blow difficult for my wife to bear. Even worse, whenever Jezzy did something Hester didn't like, which was frequent, my wife blamed me because it was my mother doing it. So, in an ironic twist of fate, Ahab and Jezzy's happiness came at the direct expense of Hester's and mine. This added immeasurable grief to our conflicted marriage.

If you think I'm overstating the situation, just think about it for a minute. When my mother married Hester's father, my wife also became my stepsister and I became her stepbrother. Despite the fact that we were not blood relatives or kin in any way, I was sleeping with my sister. Although, being a man, this didn't bother me in the slightest; it definitely bothered Hester. She flinched at the idea of being intimate with her brother. Obviously, I wasn't literally her brother, but she made an issue about our bizarre situation for quite a while. Maybe it was just the right reason for her to be cold to me.

Frankly, I was glad to see my mother move to New England. Once they were gone—now more than a thousand miles away—things settled down quite a bit, but it didn't start out that way. Honestly, if my dad and her mother had died several years earlier and Hester and I become stepsister and stepbrother, I doubt we would have ever become man and wife. In fact, I'm sure of it.

To me, the entire situation seemed a little incestuous. For obvious reasons, I never admitted this to my wife.

As young as they were, it was also bizarre and confusing to our kids. One of my children, on more than one occasion, had asked me if I had married my sister. This made Hester and me feel like perverts. Sometimes our kids thought it was cute, often giggling about our bizarre situation. Perhaps the only people who could possibly understand how we felt are those living in the Ozarks or Appalachia. I hear such things are common there.

When you are young, you can adapt to most anything. That didn't make our situation healthy though. The roles for everybody in our family became blurred and slightly out of focus. Because Hester and I were man and wife while simultaneously being brother and sister, our boundaries were totally out of whack. Having married so young, we looked to our parents for support, especially when we began to grow our family. It became hard for us to look to them for support when our parents became our in-laws.

Not knowing which hat our parents were wearing at any given time, many things baffled us. Others produced conflicts that made our lives unnecessarily difficult. Because Hester's and my relationship was strained on our best days and a nightmare on our worst, our interaction with Jezzy and Ahab became infrequent. In fact, Hester started referring to her new mother as Jezzy Ringler.

The years that followed with Hester were quite an adventure. I could write a book about what happened. In fact, I intend to do just that, but that story will have to wait. What I have divulged so far is just background information. All of it was mentioned in order for you to understand what happened.

Now, we are going to move rather quickly through the next fifteen years.

Chapter 7

Acts of Perfidy

When marriages start out being as difficult as Hester's and mine, they occasionally settle down to become very fulfilling. More often than not, however, the disharmony that exists escalates rather than dissipates. Despite the fact that we had five children together, our marriage was tumultuous shortly after we first married and continued to be that way until Hester filed for divorce in 2000.

From the day I fell in love with her, when I was just eighteen and she was still sixteen, my feelings for her never changed. I loved her, but my love was not reciprocated. My wife needed me because we had five children. Her commitment to me was because I was a good provider—not because I was her beloved mate. This isn't the way I wanted things to be between us, but I was powerless in making her respond differently. The threat of her leaving me was a constant fear I was forced to live with. That never changed. As you can imagine, I had abandonment issues. These issues magnified the existing abandonment issues originating from the time my mother packed my bag and almost gave me up for adoption.

That Hester used my weakness against me and manipulated me with it is evidence of exactly how unhealthy our marriage was. If I didn't do what she wanted, exactly when she wanted it, she threatened to leave me. It was her ace of trumps knowing I would inevitably cave to her relentless demands. It didn't matter if her demands were in the best interests of our family or not. Over the years, this happened hundreds, maybe thousands of times. I wish I was exaggerating but I'm not.

Her threat to leave, divorce me and take my children away was an ever-present part of our marriage. I lived in constant fear of it. Living like this exacted a terrible emotional toll on me. Being married to Hester eroded my sense of being a worthwhile human being—much like the constant drip of Chinese water torture, Instead of being confident and self-assured, like my father was, I became timid and fearful. Never able to rest and enjoy my marriage, I routinely went to extreme measures to try and please my wife. The only thing that seemed to work was buying things for her, but this only pacified the situation for a short while. Then, just like the turning tide, things would revert back and she would belittle and browbeat me.

That I took it, accepting her contempt and disapproval as valid, shows exactly how weak my moral foundation had become. Hester was committed to crushing my spirit. I could go on and on about how she was cruel and how her actions were unjustified, but I have to admit that I allowed her to treat me the way she did.

It is difficult for me to admit this because it's so emasculating— but it's the truth. Sadly, I continued to submit myself to this self-destructive, subservient way of existing throughout our marriage. The only respite from her constant badgering and hateful attitude came when I would indulge her materialistic cravings with lavish presents, especially clothing and fine jewelry. There was a reason I was able to satisfy my wife's desires this way.

Although she considered me to be a complete failure as a husband, outside of the home I was an entirely different person. Despite starting out as a construction worker, being paid by the hour, I was good at what I did and I learned to seize unique opportunities when they presented themselves. Even with five children to feed, I did quite well for our family and became quite successful. This may seem surprising to you, especially since I was still quite young and never went to college, but I was fairly affluent by the time I was in my mid-twenties.

The year after my father died, which was the year before my mother-in-law passed, I began a crane rental company in the construction industry. That happened in 1983 when I was just twenty-two years old. Although it was a struggle to make ends meet when I began the company, my efforts began to pay off. By the time I sold the company three years later, when I was just twenty-five, I had made a substantial profit. Plus, I learned a key lesson in life—how to make money.

By the time I sold the company, we already had four of our five children. Because they were all still young, Hester needed me more than she wanted to get rid of me. So our marriage limped along like this for years with each of us unfulfilled. The one thing she did like about me was that I was no longer dirt poor. Always wanting to be a man of means like my father-in-law/stepfather, having back pocket money made me feel good about myself. Especially since I was never validated at home.

In 1986, I started another construction company and it also did quite well. Even though I was just twenty-five at the time, my company took off. This made us quite affluent. She loved this, of course, but like the *sword of Damocles*, the threat of being abandoned was always held over my head.

As our children began growing up, going to school and being involved in afterschool activities, we settled down to a semi-normal family life. Having substantial discretionary income to spend, all generated by me, pleased Hester. It didn't make me attractive to her, but it was enough to hold the family together—at least for a while.

In 1989, I started a second business—a marketing business—and Hester became my business partner. We became Amway

Distributors and were extraordinarily successful with it. Eventually we became Diamond Distributors. In the Amway food chain, this meant we were making quite a bit of money and were positioned to make much more. What I liked best about it was it seemed to bring Hester and me closer together. We traveled together to speak to enthusiastic crowds quite often. We told them about how they could also grow their businesses and make money— just like we had. The experience was positive for both of us and Hester loved being in the limelight. She especially liked wearing fashionable clothes, expensive shoes and ornate jewelry.

I had hoped our success in Amway might help us turn the corner with our relationship and it actually did for a while—quite a while. Nevertheless, things fell apart again eight years later. In 1997, she left me and moved to Spartanburg, South Carolina. She wanted to be closer to her father and my mother. Several years earlier, Ahab and Jezzy had moved there for business reasons of their own. They seemed to be doing very well. Naturally, I was devastated by this turn of events. Being abandoned again— just like I had been when Hester was pregnant with our first son—was devastating. Without my wife and children around me, I floundered badly. For the first time, I understood exactly how Ahab must have felt when his wife died. Being alone, he didn't know what to do with himself; neither did I.

Not knowing what else to do and not nearly ready to accept the inevitability of divorce, I repeatedly begged Hester to come back. Taking my vow to remain married to her for life seriously, I almost became obsessed with staying married. Regardless of what it required, I wanted to keep our family together.

Despite the fact that I had been very successful—both as a contractor and as a marketer for Amway—it meant nothing to me without my family. I started a home building business while simultaneously doing my best to woo my estranged wife. I was successful with both endeavors. Because I knew what I was doing in the construction business, I felt certain

I would succeed. Restoring my relationship with Hester was much more problematic. She came back but she never really put her feet down.

Three years later she left me again. In 2000, she moved back to Washington with our kids, leaving me in Spartanburg. I was left close to where Ahab and Jezzy lived. Somehow, this seemed ironic. When she left to return to Washington, Hester said she wanted to be closer to one of her sisters. I think she just wanted to get as far away from me as possible. This time, when she left, she filed for divorce.

Continuing with my predictable pattern, I begged her to come back, but she was immovable. By this time, having been married for twenty years and having our children so early in our marriage, several of them were nearly grown. My oldest daughter, Olivia, was close to being engaged to a youth pastor, Jared Prynne. He was from our denomination and had asked me if I would approve of them marrying. Although nine years older than Olivia, they seemed well suited for each other.

Since he was practically family, Jared offered to help me resolve my issues with Hester. He indicated that if I purged my soul by making a full confession of my sins, Hester might be forgiving and we might be able to reconcile before our divorce became final.

Agreeing to intercede, Jared traveled across the country to meet with me. Our meeting was long and very difficult for me emotionally. Jared, who was acting as my confessor, encouraged me to make a full and complete declaration of guilt about all of my transgressions, including everything I was feeling about my estranged wife. Before I got down on my knees to pray, he told me that God would honor my confession.

Being desperate to do anything that might help me reconcile with Hester, I opened up my heart and my history to my future son-in-law. I disclosed everything, precisely the way a penitent should while making my confession.

When I was finished, he looked at me and said, "That's not good enough, Steve—not nearly good enough. You have to dig deeper, much deeper."

A little surprised, I did as he instructed. I told him exactly how angry I had been about numerous situations throughout Hester's and my long and tumultuous marriage. With twenty years of frustration built up inside of me, my anger and resentment toward her just seemed to pour out. Once my cathartic confession was complete, I felt drained—totally spent—but my soul experienced relief.

Not long afterwards, I made a special trip to Washington to make one final plea to Hester. I had to try and win her back one more time. Before flying west, she agreed to meet me at a local *Olive Garden* Restaurant for lunch. Once I arrived, I asked to be seated at a corner table where I had a flower arrangement placed. I also picked out a spot with a view—one I knew she would like. I wanted everything to be perfect and it was.

She was supposed to arrive at 11:30 a.m., but she didn't show. I waited patiently. By noon, the waitress said I would have to order or relinquish the table. I asked for a few more minutes hoping Hester would arrive, but it looked like I had made a cross-country trip for nothing. Finally, at 12:15, forty-five minutes later, she walked in. I stood to welcome her, but she had no intention of sitting or of having lunch with me.

Instead, in a voice loud enough for every patron in the restaurant to hear, she yelled, "I hate you. Can't you get that through your thick head, Steve? I want a f*@!/*! divorce!"

Having said her piece, she didn't wait for me to reply. Instead, she turned around and walked out of the restaurant leaving me completely humiliated. Placing a generous tip on the table for the waitress, I gathered my things and walked out a couple of minutes after Hester. Every eye in the place followed me out of the restaurant, which was very embarrassing. I felt like a serial killer—or worse. It was a horrible experience, to say the least.

When I reached my car, I expected Hester to be long gone. She wasn't. She was right there, standing next to my parked car. Looking me straight in the eye, she said, "Do you really want to do something to save our marriage?"

"Yes, I'll do anything," I responded—just like she knew I would.

"Okay," she replied, mellowing a little. "What I need is for you to go shopping with me. I want you to buy the kids and me some new clothes. Are you willing to do that?"

"Of course, I am," I acknowledged.

Although hungry, not having eaten lunch, we headed off to the mall on a shopping spree. Several hours later, once she had spent a small fortune decking herself out, plus buying a few items for our children, she turned to me and said, "Jared needs some new clothes too. I want you to buy them for him. Will you?"

"Absolutely," I replied without hesitation. It did mean that Hester would spend more time with me though and I hoped my generosity would make a difference—but it didn't. She went ahead with the divorce. Nothing I said or did altered her resolve to get rid of me. Needless to say, I felt used, which was crushing.

———◇———

At our divorce hearing, I was surprised my future son-in-law, Jared Prynne, had actually transcribed every word I said during my confession. He had encouraged me to confess my sins. He emphasized that it was a prerequisite before Hester and I could reconcile, but it was all a con.

His purpose wasn't to help me. Instead, what I confessed became the primary evidence Hester used against me to gain custody of our children. This act of betrayal, instigated by Jared and Hester offended me and left me embittered towards them. The entire episode was so distasteful, sinister and calculated. Hester was in league with our youth minister to destroy me and had manipulated me into betraying myself. When I purchased several outfits for Jared at the mall, I didn't feel good about it, but I went ahead and bought the clothes anyway to appease my wife. After having spent so much money on her and our kids, I reasoned that it wouldn't hurt to spend a little more on a young man who had made such an effort to help me reconcile with my wife. This was the last time I saw Hester before we were in court.

After having been used so badly by my daughter's boyfriend, at the behest of his future mother-in-law, I cannot tell you how angry it made me. What I can tell you is that their plan to ensnare and destroy me was effective. Hester gained full custody and I was saddled with hefty monthly payments for child support.

When I returned to South Carolina, I felt defeated—completely vanquished by the self-serving, cunning wiles of my ex-wife. But her treachery was not complete—not by a long shot. Within six months before our divorce was final, Jared, my soon-to-be son-in-law and our family youth pastor, broke off his relationship with my oldest daughter. He then became involved with my ex-wife, Hester. When this began, I don't know, but I certainly have my suspicions. Although Hester was nine years older than Jared, she apparently had no problem breaching boundaries with her potential future son-in-law and man of the cloth.

I didn't think anything could surprise me, but Hester's cunning ruthlessness and taking up with Jared certainly did. I was flabbergasted. On the other hand, it also gave me great insight into the character of the woman I had been married to for twenty years. Not long thereafter, Jared and my ex-wife married, becoming Hester and Jared Prynne. When I learned this, another piece of the puzzle fell into place. I finally understood who Hester was and what her intention toward me had been all along. Although shocked to hear the news, I wasn't surprised by how deeply deceitful she had been. My sense of betrayal was profound—not just for me but also for my daughter.

I felt worse for my precious daughter, Olivia, than I did for myself. Young, naive and innocent, she didn't deserve what happened to her. I couldn't imagine how she felt knowing that her own mother had seduced her serious boyfriend. I couldn't fathom a mother betraying her own child like that. What kind of woman would do such a thing? Hester's duplicity was beyond anything I would ever have imagined she could do. Such a betrayal is beyond words.

Once we were divorced and my pain began to diminish, Hester's spell over me finally broke. She had cast it upon me when I was just eighteen—a kid really—but that was then and things had changed. Not yet forty and recently divorced, my life was about to begin anew and I was ready for whatever might come to pass. At least I thought I was.

Chapter 8

Rock Bottom

ester, with the help of her lover, who became her husband soon thereafter, was completely victorious in her war against me. In the zero sum game of divorce, she was the undisputed winner. The outcome was a foregone conclusion before the proceedings even commenced. Although I didn't realize it at the time, I never had a chance.

From her twisted perspective—one in which she never did anything wrong—she was actually doing "God's will" by divorcing me and had been proclaiming this boldly. Resigned to my fate, I assumed that Hester would do the right thing and the dissolution of our marriage would be finalized honorably. I took for granted that everything would be fair and on the up-and-up. Of course it wasn't.

My mistake was huge and it cost me dearly. From the day Hester made the decision to divorce me, her goal was to take everything from me—my money, my good name, and my self-worth. She was successful at achieving her goal and triumphant beyond her wildest aspirations. I despised the fact that I had been victimized by her calculated treachery—all in the "name of God."

My heart was completely broken in a way few people understand. This is a place not everyone divorced has experienced, I felt my heart break, leaving a numbing feeling through my body and mind mixed with emotional pain I have no words to describe. I wondered what the meaning of life really was as I was going into the unknown valley filled with the shadows of rejection and loss. Many times I drove to church and could not go in after hearing the whispers of gossip and the looks of distain for a divorced man, this was completely unacceptable in the church culture at the time. After losing more than fifty pounds and not sleeping more than a few hours at a time, I decided to start running—and run I did. It was the only relief I could find as I played worship music to fill my mind as the miles went behind me. I also found comfort in psalms, reading them I realized the Lord has not forgotten me and others have suffered also. I started over alone and financially broke at forty years old.

But with the help of a counselor I started to see things differently.

Although we had been married for twenty years, I never really knew who she was. Once I came to understand her better, my perspective about our marriage changed. Being out of her life, on a day-to-day basis anyway, I was no longer the fall guy and was free to be myself.

Despite my newfound clarity, my life was not easy. I found it especially difficult being alone. It was my constant fear. I finally had to deal with my abandonment issues and work through them, which I was able to do in counseling. The bad news was that I was all alone for over a decade. It actually took years to start feeling good about myself.

My court-ordered monthly payments to Hester were exorbitant. Because of this, I had no choice but to put my nose to the grindstone and work even harder. It's a good thing I liked to work. To support my children and myself, I started a home building business in the Spartanburg area of South Carolina— just north of Greenville.

Since the area was growing, I did quite well. This kept me busy and it also kept my mind off of how unfairly I had been treated. As my business grew, it became prosperous and I became affluent once again. Even though my child support was high, my greatest expense—maintaining Hester's lavish, indulged lifestyle—was no longer my responsibility.

As my business prospered, my family began to heal. One by one, beginning with Olivia, my kids left the Pacific Northwest to come live with me in Greer, South Carolina. I welcomed each of them with open arms. My youngest child Daniel, who was too young to decide which parent to live with, was the only one who stayed with his mother and stepdad. When Daniel came to visit, it was wonderful until it was time to send him back to Washington. This was a sight to see at the airport only three years old as he would cry and say he didn't want to leave me! I would fight to hold back the tears until he was out of site. Often, I would see strangers cry to witness this gruesome process. He was flying alone, and as an unaccompanied minor, an assigned flight attendant assisted him.

Although Hester had won the courtroom battle, she ended up losing the war. Our children, being pawns in the battle, began to see things the way they really were. Hester hadn't taken this into consideration. When you use deceptive means to gain an advantage, what you receive are the just fruits of the deceit you initiate. Being repudiated by her children was the cost Hester was forced to pay for her underhanded behavior and it was a hefty price to pay.

By using Olivia's boyfriend to destroy me, which hurt my daughter very badly, Hester also alienated her second oldest child. Watching the bizarre and unwholesome drama unfold, Olivia's siblings saw things for what they were. And they were appalled. They didn't like what had happened and they didn't like the role Jared was playing in hurting their father.

Hester assumed that Jared would just come in, sleep in my bed, and become their new stepfather. Unfortunately for her, none of my kids wanted anything to do with him. Plus, they loathed the circumstances at home.

Olivia was the child most affected by Hester's deception. Obviously, my oldest daughter couldn't live in the same house with her ex-boyfriend sleeping with her mother. That Hester and Jared thought Olivia was capable of accepting such behavior—and being okay with it—was mindboggling. It was beyond my ability to conceive, but neither Hester nor Jared factored this into their equation. Perhaps their lust blinded them to the reality of how negatively their relationship would be viewed by our trusting children.

To me, knowing how Hester operated, this was the only explanation that made sense. Regardless of what Hester and Jared's thinking happened to be, there was no way Olivia could continue to live in such an unhealthy environment. So, she packed up her belongings—and called me to move her back home. Once she was in South Carolina, she flourished.

When they were young, one of my kids favorite shows was *Romper Room*. They loved it, but certainly didn't enjoy the adult version, starring their mother and their youth minister. So, just like Olivia, the others followed suit and left their mother behind in Washington, one at a time. My youngest daughter demanded a change in custody allowing her to live permanently with her father. I did not get involved in this, what happened is Hester voluntarily gave up her daughter in the same court the custody battle was fought and she lived with me until she was grown and married.

With all of my children, except for my youngest, eventually living with me, I settled down to finish raising my kids as a single parent.

Although she achieved what she wanted, my crushing defeat actually became an overwhelming victory. The way everything in my life unfolded proves that there is no right way to do a wrong thing. It's a lesson I hope Hester will learn one day.

As a dad, I was successful but it wasn't easy. Being a single parent never is. My work also thrived and I made a great deal of money during that period building houses in such a high growth area of the Palmetto State. Because my children came to live with me, my only expense to her was for the child support of my youngest son, Daniel.

This meant that I was able to save quite a bit of money. Eventually, in 2004, I sold my home building business in the Spartanburg area at a substantial profit. Having capital to invest, I began making some real estate deals in Charleston and Myrtle Beach. Although the area in which we lived was growing, the Low Country was growing much faster. Numerous people from up North retired to South Carolina and many more were predicted to come. A slew of baby-boomers were about to retire, which meant that housing would be at a premium. There was a lot of money to be made in the Charleston area and I wanted some of it to be mine. The deal I eventually made, however, proved to be the worst decision of my life—even worse than my mistakes with Hester.

Chapter 9

What My Father Warned Me About

W hen you are married to someone for a long time, as I was to Hester, especially having five children together, your ex-spouse never exits your life completely. Most divorces are like this and my relationship with Hester was no different, Her impact on me did diminish and I considered this to be a good thing.

The less I had to do with her the better. Clearly, our divorce was more difficult for our kids to accept than it was for their parents, but they were remarkably resilient. Once they were in South Carolina with me, they reconnected with their old friends and made some new ones. They became active in school events and also enjoyed all of the youth activities available for them at our church. All of this helped them heal—at least as much as kids ever heal from a divorce. Despite the trauma of having their family ripped apart, our lives were busy and full.

Hester wasn't the only Dimesdale I had to deal with, though. Although Ahab was no longer my father-in-law, he was still my stepfather and the grandfather of my children. Not to mention, we lived in the same town and within very close proximity to each other.

Ahab was one of the most respected and revered men in the Apostolic Lutheran denomination and he was universally admired because of how successful he had been in business. He enjoyed the good life as well as his elevated stature within our denomination for as long as I could remember. Nevertheless, as is so often true, there was a vast difference between appearance and reality. Although Ahab and Jezzy continued to look the part of the consummate power couple, most of it had become superficial. Having made several poor investments, Ahab no longer had the resources he once had to sustain his lavish lifestyle. He also wasn't willing to downsize. Although few knew it, myself included, he wasn't just broke. He was also heavily in debt.

Fortunately for me, I wasn't. Having sold my business for a substantial profit and having made several wise investments, I had become quite comfortable again. I wasn't rich, but I was very affluent. Even better, things continued to improve for me. While I was heading up in the world, Ahab's fortunes were declining precipitously.

Both my mother and my stepfather were well aware of my recent successes. Seeing an advantage and wanting to change the course of their own downward trajectory, they sought me out.

One day, out of the blue, I received a call from my stepfather.

"Mornin', Steve," Ahab said pleasantly, knowing I would recognize his voice instantly.

"Hi, Ahab," I responded respectfully.

"I hope you and the kids are doing okay?" Ahab asked.

"We're doing great. How are you and Mom?" I asked, keeping the conversation light.

"Couldn't be better," he responded with a chuckle. "That's one of the reasons I'm calling. Now that all of the unpleasantness of your divorce is behind us, I sure would like for our families to get closer together, wouldn't you?" Since he asked his question rhetorically, knowing how I would answer, he continued without allowing me to reply. "Your mom wants to spend more time with her grandchildren and so do I."

"I'm sure the kids would like that," I added.

"One way we might be able to accomplish that goal is if you and I were in business together," he continued, taking the conversation in an entirely different direction. This was obviously the real reason for his call. After floating out this possibility, he waited for me to respond, which I did immediately.

"I think it would be great for all of us to get together more often Ahab, but there is no way I want to be in business with you." Allowing what I said to sink in for a second, I added: "Besides, I like doing things on my own and I'm doing pretty well as it is."

"I know you are, Steve, and I'm so proud of you for all you have accomplished. From the time you were a teenager, back when you asked Hester to marry you, I knew you were going to be successful. You had a fire in you then and I could see it. You still do," he added, doing his best to be ingratiating.

Being positively affirmed by my stepfather was new territory for me—that's for sure. He rarely had anything good to say about me, but it did let me know that something was definitely up with him.

Responding to the real issue, I said, "I don't know, Ahab. Being in business with a family member is never a good idea."

Laughing heartily, he said, "You don't even know what the deal is, Steve! At least hear me out. Will you do that?"

"Sure," I said. But I already knew I wouldn't be interested, regardless of what he had in mind.

"There's a piece of property on James Island, right across the drawbridge off of 17, heading out of Charleston. It's directly across the street from the Piggly Wiggly Shopping Center. Do you know the spot I'm talking about?"

Having shopped a few times at that Piggly Wiggly, I pictured the location in my mind's eye. Answering Ahab, I said, "Yes,

I think I do. If you went straight, you would end up at Folly Beach. If you turned right, after cutting through the golf course, you would eventually end up on John's Island. Am I right?"

"You are exactly right, Steve. Anyway, right now, the land I'm talking about is raw and it's prime real estate. We can build eighty-four condos on it. The profits from this deal would set both of our families up for the rest of our lives." After a short pause, he added, "I think this is something you and I should pursue, don't you?"

When he began pressing me like this, my mind instantly returned to my wedding day nearly twenty-five years earlier. Thinking back, I remembered my father squeezing my arm, warning me about Ahab's shady deals and unscrupulous business ethics. Having been warned by my dad, I knew what I had to do.

Knowing better than to get involved with Ahab, I said, "Sorry, I know it sounds good, but that deal isn't for me."

Rather than take no for an answer, Ahab pursued me with the same vigor I had used to talk Hester into marrying me when we were teenagers. Although Ahab was relentless, I was equally immovable. He was very pushy, but he also kept sweetening the deal for me, making it more attractive each time the subject was discussed. Gradually, he began to wear down my resolve.

Finally I said, "Okay, I'll do it."

By the time I made the commitment, if everything went like he said it would, I would end up making more from the deal than I had from all of my other deals combined. The profits from it were almost too good to be true, which I should have recognized as a red flag, but didn't. All I saw was a green flag ... as in how much money there was to be made.

⌐------◇------⌐

My initial investment in the deal was $100,000. This amount was required just to hold the land. Being a fifty-fifty partner with me in the deal, it was Ahab's responsibility to equal that amount, but he couldn't. Although he said he intended to match my earnest money soon thereafter, he admitted to me that he was a little low on cash. Assuring me he would match it soon, he also promised to pay ten percent interest for the time he was delinquent. With no other choice, believing the deal was a good one, I put up the money in 2005 and secured the property.

In 2006, we closed on the property, which meant that I was required to put up an additional $200,000. Ahab was required to put up $200,000 as well, plus the $100,000 he still hadn't paid. He was still short on cash. Although we were fifty-fifty partners, I had already put up $300,000 and Ahab hadn't put up a dime. He kept saying he would, but he was always evasive about it.

By that point, however, with $300,000 already committed to the deal, I was obligated to the project—tied to it irrevocably. I didn't like what was happening but I was as bound to it as I had been to Ahab's daughter when I married her. Although Hester and I were equally yoked in one way, Ahab and I were joined at the hip in another way—as business partners. My entire situation with Ahab felt eerily familiar and the feeling wasn't pleasant. It felt as though I had the entire financial burden, while neither Hester nor Ahab ever paid anything. Both enjoyed the fruits of my labor seemingly for free.

Real estate development is an interesting business. Taking raw land and building eighty-four condominiums on it doesn't happen overnight. It takes a while. In our case, the process required several years. This meant funds for our operation weren't needed weekly or even monthly. When funds were required, however, large amounts needed to be spent.

Unfortunately, where money was concerned, this is where I came in. So far, I had paid the earnest money while Ahab had yet to meet any of his obligations.

Before we closed on the property, we needed a contractor to actually construct the buildings. We didn't choose a man who came highly recommended. Instead, Ahab's son, James, who was a general contractor and my stepbrother, got the job. This complicated matters further, as you can imagine. James had an equity position, but he didn't get it for free. We offered him a piece of the action for $400,000, based on the increased value of the project. For his investment, Ahab gave him ten percent of his equity. I did too. Like Ahab though, all of James's cash was tied up, so he didn't actually write a check. He just promised to do so in the future.

Because the magnitude and scope of our project was escalating, we needed to protect ourselves by forming a corporation. One day, while I was surveying the property, I saw a pelican sitting on a branch overlooking the bay. The bird was majestic but also seemed calm and serene. When I saw the bird who looked like he was watching over our property, protecting it, I thought, *Why don't we name our company, Pelican Gulf?*

When I told Ahab and James about it, both of them loved the idea, concurring immediately. The name of our partnership became Pelican Gulf, LLC. We formed it because all of us needed to protect our personal assets.

Everything about the project was proceeding nicely except the fact that I was the only one who had actually put up any cash. All I received from Ahab and James were promises and excuses—lots of them.

Because neither of their situations improved when it came time to close on the bank loan, both scrambled to find the money they needed to complete the deal. At the time, because Pelican Gulf was run through the construction company, they wrote all of the checks. I wasn't involved in the day-to-day operations. That made me an investor.

When it came time to close, our lending institution required me, along with Ahab and James, to guarantee the repayment of the funds personally. The loan to finance the construction of the eighty-four condos was $13.2 million and I had to guarantee this burden separately—so did Ahab and James. Each of us was on the hook for $13.2 million. This was a lot of money.

I didn't like this situation one bit. Having been involved in real estate development since I was twenty, I knew this might happen, so I discussed this possibility with Ahab before I ever committed to do the deal. He assured me that this would never happen, but it did. Now, three years later, the bank wouldn't proceed with the loan unless I signed for the funds personally. With no choice in the matter and without losing the project and my $300,000, I signed, but I resented having done so.

Completely aware of my financial vulnerability, I signed the papers, hoping for the best. Nevertheless, my father's admonition to stay away from any financial deals with Ahab kept ringing in my ears. I tried to remain optimistic and upbeat about the future, but it was difficult. I could no longer dismiss the terrible sense of foreboding that gripped my stomach and troubled my heart. My days were filled with apprehension. Fearful about what the future might be, my mind raced at night and robbed me of sleep.

Chapter 10

Weakness and Greed

W hen Hester and I divorced, it finally became clear to me that everything about how our marriage ended was devious and manipulative. Nothing was straightforward and honest, as I erroneously assumed it would be.

Unlike most contentious divorces, where wounded spouses regularly lash out at one another by using high-priced lawyers— like having a surrogate bully verbally beat up a bad spouse— couples have no other purpose than to hurt their estranged partner. This wasn't Hester's goal. Her purpose was far more sinister and underhanded than something as simple as that. Her aim was to annihilate me totally. She wanted to take my money, my children and my good name—in that order. Nothing short of complete victory would suffice. For Hester, our divorce was a zero-sum game with one victor and one loser—and that's exactly how she played it.

For quite some time, she was very successful at achieving her goal. As the reality of what had happened began to dawn on me, I came to understand just how naive I had been. Finally, I admitted to myself just how conniving she had been.

I should have learned from this very painful and expensive mistake, but I didn't. Where Hester was concerned, I had been a fool and it cost me. That she was her father's daughter and had adopted his twisted value system should have kept me from ever getting involved with Ahab in a substantial business venture. My father had warned me against it.

You know the old adage, "Fool me once, shame on you; fool me twice, shame on me"—or "once burned, twice cautious." Both were applicable, but I had ignored them.

Although I suspected things were not completely on the up-and-up, Ahab assured me that they were. Everything about this deal went against my better judgment. I obviously hadn't learned my lesson, which was to stay away from any dealings with the Dimesdale family for the rest of my life.

Although never completely comfortable being Ahab's partner, I allowed my greed to trump my discernment. Again, that's on me, but Ahab knew how to use my weakness to his advantage— just like Hester did. Embracing the idea of being very affluent— just like Ahab had been his entire life—I closed my eyes to each of the potential dangers and stepped into the trap that had been carefully set to ensnare me.

When we closed on the loan, we picked up a check from the bank for our first draw. It provided us with all of the operating capital we would need to complete the project of building eighty-four condominiums. Quite a while after closing the deal, I received a check from our corporation, Pelican Gulf, LLC, for my investment of $300,000. Obviously, this was a relief.

Having this much cash tied up for so long had become a real burden. I was relieved to be reimbursed, but I was still on the hook for the entire $13.2 million if our project went south for any reason. I understood this, of course, but I forced myself to be optimistic about what the future held. I also did my best to repress my apprehensiveness, but I was only moderately successful at doing so.

Ahab and his son, James, also received checks for their part of the down payment. Ahab's original investment, like mine, was $300,000, and Herman's was $400,000. Although I didn't learn about what happened when we closed on the property—not until several years later—neither of them put in their full share. They certainly didn't inform me about this. I would have been livid and might not have gone through with the deal. They knew that, of course, so they chose to deceive me. It was just like the true purpose for my confession to the youth minister several years earlier. Hester had kept me in the dark about what was really happening back then too.

Based on the amount they paid themselves back, I was sure that Ahab had only put up $180,000. His son had put up only $99,980—much less than what was required. Had I known this up front, I'm not sure what I would have done. Having never been told the truth, I wasn't given the option.

Had this been the only financial irregularity, it would have been one thing—especially since we all recovered our initial capital. Unfortunately it wasn't. This was just the opening salvo in a financial deal that was never straightforward and honest. Although it was financial betrayal by my stepfather and stepbrother, I felt much the same way Olivia must have felt when her own mother who seduced her boyfriend away from her had felt.

I had no idea any of this was happening because I was being purposefully kept in the dark by my partners. I hoped that at least my mother, being married to Ahab, would look out for me. I could count on her. I was certain she wouldn't allow me to be used, abused and then discarded by her husband and stepson. What mother would?

Despite my suspicions, which I thought might be without merit, I continued to sit passively hoping for the best. I was like Neville Chamberlain, who kept his head in the sand until it was too late. I did the same thing with Ahab and James and it cost me dearly. Although I didn't know it at the time, my personal war had already commenced.

In the Scriptures, the apostle Paul discusses being content during times of plenty and times of need. Unfortunately many people are incapable of embracing such a lifestyle. Ahab certainly wasn't. Having had enormous discretionary income his entire life and spending as he saw fit, he was simply incapable of downsizing his lifestyle to live within his means. Neither was his wife, my mother, Jezzy. She loved being affluent nearly as much as she loved him.

Continuing to enjoy the lavish standard of living they had been accustomed to since marrying two decades earlier, Ahab persisted in spending more than he earned. In fact, his expenses exceeded his income by quite a bit. Even then, he refused to reign in his spending. The only solution to his financial problems was to earn more money.

Desperate to regain his fortune, he made one bad business decision after the other. As a result, his financial situation continued to decline at an alarming rate. Needing immediate cash to prevent going belly up, he began taking from our partnership, Pelican Gulf, LLC.

Since he and his son kept the books, I was unaware of what was transpiring. Although I wasn't a silent partner—not completely—being a single dad, I was very busy raising my kids in Spartanburg. Consequently, I wasn't part of the day-to-day operations of Pelican Gulf on James Island. I didn't know what they were really doing.

Hoping I would never discover the truth, which I didn't for quite a while, Ahab took at least $300,000 out of the corporation. He used this money to undergird his lavish way of life. He did this without informing me. Essentially, he embezzled the money. And that's not all that he did. Ahab also borrowed one million dollars from Shamus O'Dunnigan—a man he had been doing business with long before I ever married Hester or had anything to do with the Dimesdale family. My father knew about Shamus and the shady business dealings he had had with

Ahab. Perhaps Shamus was the person my dad was thinking about when he warned me about Ahab's unscrupulous business dealings.

I knew Shamus, but not well. He was the person who originally discovered the piece of land on James Island where Pelican Gulf was about to build eighty-four condominiums. As a finder's fee for bringing us the deal, the corporation paid Shamus a large sum of money. The way the deal was structured, Shamus was given $200,000 in cash and four condos, which could be valued at more than the one million dollars.

After all, Shamus was his old friend and they had been doing business with each other for decades. It was a personal loan and nothing to do with Pelican or me. It was solidified with a handshake. As far as I knew, there was no paperwork accompanying the loan.

Ahab didn't use any of the proceeds to repay what he had embezzled from our company though. He needed everything he got—just to keep his head above water. He actually needed more than what he embezzled and borrowed, but what he had gave him some breathing room. Although it's hard to imagine, this is precisely how deep a hole Ahab had dug for himself.

On the surface, the funds Ahab received, especially the loan, might appear to be his problem and have nothing to do with me. This is how it should have been, but it wasn't. It eventually became my problem too.

The web of lies Ahab had woven just to maintain his indulgent lifestyle came to impact me in profound ways that I could never have foreseen or imagined at the time. Although a sense of foreboding was always present, I remained blissfully unaware of what was about to happen—clueless about how devastating it would be.

Meanwhile, although there was so much transpiring under the table, on the surface, everything seemed to be going very well. Construction on the condos had begun and it was moving along nicely. Superficially, everything looked great—at least to me. The project was being completed on time and within budget. The skies ahead looked clear, but this was an illusion. Just behind the horizon, a dark cloud was forming that produced a tornado of seismic proportions. Although I didn't know it at the time, it would toss me about like a straw in the wind.

Chapter 11

A Storm Is Brewing

Desperate people are capable of doing almost anything. Some are more rash than others and go on to live their lives recklessly. This was the case where Ahab was concerned. He embezzled lots of money from our corporation. What he was doing had catastrophic ramifications because he wasn't just stealing from the business and from myself, he was breaking the law. What he was doing also increased the pressure on him to "make something happen."

Now that he had committed a felony, he knew he had to put the funds back before his illegal behavior became public knowledge. He probably thought he could just get away with it and not suffer any negative repercussions. I suppose this is what all white-collar criminals believe.

Since I was the injured party and his stepson, he probably wasn't as worried as he would have been if Pelican Gulf had been a public company. Being a family owned business might have provided him with the justification he needed to take the money. And since he was the head of the family—at least in his own eyes—he felt he could do what he wanted. I'm not certain how he twisted reality to justify his criminal behavior. I do know that Ahab kept what he had done carefully hidden from me. Obviously, he wasn't proud of what he had been doing.

I had no idea that anything illegal was going on. I was nervous about what had already transpired though. Who wouldn't be? Looking back, I'm not sure how I should have reacted to his theft. I doubt I would have gone to the police at that point, but I would have made sure those funds were taken out of Ahab's share of Pelican Gulf's future earnings. Ahab was obviously worried enough about what my reaction would be that he made sure to cover his tracks. He did a good job of it too. I remained in the dark for quite a while—but not forever.

The one million dollars Ahab borrowed from Shamus O'Dunnigan brought a "wild card" player into our lives. He probably thought he could control my reaction to his embezzlement if his crime had been uncovered. As for Shamus and controlling his reaction, that would be a different story.

Originally from the Boston area, Shamus was as Irish as they came. He even drank *Jameson* whiskey. He always had a bottle of it around just in case he needed a sip or two. Sporting a winning smile, Shamus loved to tell jokes that were lewd, off color and often racist. He thought everyone who heard them thought they were cute. If someone was offended, which happened often, he didn't care. In fact, he would even tell another offensive joke. This is just the way he was.

A consummate bully, he was "in your face" about everything. It was like he had arrested development. It seemed as if his behavior never progressed past his sophomore year of high school. To me, he resembled a mean-spirited version of Fonzie from *Happy Days*.

Although nearly seventy-years-old, Shamus was still a powerful, virile man and he made sure anybody around him was aware of just how imposing he could be. I only met him a few times. He was always pleasant to me, which wasn't surprising. After all, if I hadn't put down the original investment of $100,000, he would never have received his finder's fee valued at one million dollar. Now that I think about it, if someone was responsible for providing me with that kind of money, I would be nice to that person, too.

Shamus wasn't nice to everybody, though. He certainly wasn't a quality human being. In fact, he exhibited numerous gangster-like character qualities. I have found that most people who want to be liked and accepted behave in a way that is pleasing to others. Sometimes they go to great lengths to be ingratiating. Shamus wasn't like that. He wasn't warm and pleasing. He didn't necessarily want or need people to like him. He preferred for them to fear him. He instilled fear by saying things that intimidated people.

Not surprising, his hero was the Boston criminal Whitey Bolger. Whitey is perhaps the most infamous criminal in the Bay State's history. Shamus even tried to look like Whitey and was remarkably successful at doing so. Rough and crusty, Shamus was a mean-spirited, two-legged version of Long John Silver from *Treasure Island*. He was definitely not the kind of person you would invite into your home for Sunday dinner. Despite all of these shortcomings, he had been in my stepfather's life years longer than I had.

Having only one business dealing with Shamus, most of what I knew about him was by reputation. Obviously, this wasn't true where Ahab was concerned. Having been involved in business deals for decades, the two men knew each other quite well. Ahab was well aware of what Shamus was capable of doing. Despite the dangers that accompanied doing business with Shamus, Ahab still brought him into our lives. Like a Monday morning quarterback, I have become keenly aware of most of what transpired.

◇

During this time, Ahab's financial situation continued to deteriorate. Despite the influx of $1.3 million he received for borrowing one million dollars from Shamus and embezzling

$300,000 from Pelican Gulf, Ahab's other business interests continued to siphon away his assets. Nevertheless, he maintained his lavish lifestyle. That's a given—like it was his divine right— but it was all for show. Nothing about Ahab and Jezzy's life was real, but he continued to look the part of a "mover and shaker."

She knew the truth, of course, but she also loved the pretense. Like costume jewelry, the Dimesdales continued to act the part of a power couple, but there was nothing of substance supporting it. Ahab had lost it all, which is why he needed to borrow money from Shamus.

Not surprisingly, there was no legal documentation involved in Shamus' loan to my stepfather—at least nothing I knew about. There was never any paperwork involved in any of their dealings, which speaks volumes about the legality of their business pursuits. But it did to me. For years, the two had been doing business with each other with nothing more than a simple handshake to seal the deal. This was their only contractual commitment to one another.

While all of this was transpiring, the eighty-four units were being built. This meant the project was moving along well. In fact, the overall success of our project seemed assured. This made all of us happy. I suppose at the time I was the happiest because I was unaware of Ahab's shenanigans.

I was eagerly anticipating numerous big paydays, which should have happened seamlessly. The big paydays never came. Although the structure for the condos was strong, the business undergirding wasn't. It was like a house of cards with no foundation. Pelican Gulf wouldn't do as well as it should have with Ahab's unethical and illegal business practices.

I'm sure my stepfather thought he would be able to repay the one million dollars in short order, but that didn't happen. Most of it had been spent quickly to settle past debts or it was tied up in ventures that made it impossible for Ahab to liquefy. Although this was unfortunate for Ahab, it was his problem. It shouldn't have had anything to do with me. That it became my problem indicates just how self-centered Ahab actually was.

Although clueless about the events that were transpiring under the table, they began to impact our company and me. Shamus was having cash flow problems of his own and my stepfather couldn't repay his debt. Although he pressed Ahab for payment, the money simply wasn't there. As Shamus' own situation continued to deteriorate, he ran out of options. He couldn't use his loan to my stepfather as collateral for a loan from a bank either—not based on a handshake. No lending institution would be willing to bail Shamus out of his tight spot without real and substantial collateral.

Having run out of legitimate alternatives to regain his operating capital, Shamus was forced to come up with a creative solution to solve his problem and he did. Part of his deal with Pelican Gulf for finding the property was to be the sole owner of four of the condominiums. Being prime property and having already appreciated considerably, each was valued at $280,000. When the entire project was complete and the units had been built, each one might be worth as much as half a million dollars. Shamus couldn't wait that long though. He needed cash immediately.

By the time he needed the money, we hadn't even broken ground yet. Shamus couldn't sell any of them on the open market. All Pelican Gulf had was a deed to the property. Because the units didn't exist yet, they couldn't be sold. This didn't stop Shamus. Needing a special deal, Shamus came up with the idea of selling one of his four condos to raise cash. He pressured Ahab and my mother to buy one of his units.

Because Ahab owed Shamus so much money, my stepfather was forced to buy unit 1066 from his desperate business partner. Once again, this was done with nothing more than a simple handshake. No paperwork was involved.

There were several reasons for this. First, since the unit didn't exist at the time, it couldn't be sold legally. No paperwork could document their deal anyway. If a contract is illegal, it isn't enforceable. Second, to have created paperwork involving Pelican Gulf might have meant I would become aware of things that Ahab certainly didn't want me to discover. Finally, since a handshake is how they had always done business for years, allowing their dealings to remain outside of the legal system, to do business this way was just fine with both of them. They actually preferred it.

Once the deal was set, Shamus received nearly $200,000, which was enough to meet his immediate obligations and continue doing business. At the same time, having to come up with $200,000 put a real strain on Ahab and my mother. It was money they didn't have, which meant they were forced to replenish it immediately.

Being just as creative as Shamus, they came up with an ingenious solution. They sold the phantom unit, which they now owned to my sister, Crystal, and her husband, Clyde. Since it would be worth as much as $375,000 when complete, my benevolent stepfather and equally altruistic mother made the couple a generous offer on the property. Crystal and Clyde could own it for $325,000, with $70,000 being the down payment. Although Crystal was Jezzy's daughter and Ahab's stepdaughter, the elder Dimesdales had to make a profit on the property, right? I suspect this was their reasoning anyway.

Like the deal with Shamus, the transaction between Ahab and his stepdaughter was done with a simple handshake. Because the unit wasn't even close to completion, since we hadn't even broken ground, it was not yet ready for occupancy. This meant it still couldn't be sold legally.

Nevertheless, with a benevolent, paternal smile and with Jezzy by his side, Ahab ensured Crystal and Clyde that everything was on the up-and-up even though he knew that it wasn't. Despite the fact that there is never a right way to do a wrong thing, Ahab had done just that. My stepfather and mother also promised the buyers that the paperwork would follow once the time was right and the transaction could be made legal. This never happened.

Despite Ahab's assurance to the contrary, unit 1066 remained the property of the corporation. It would be that way until the project was complete. Although selling the phantom condo the way they did worked for Shamus, my parents and my sister, the entire transaction was done under the table. None of it was straightforward, honest or ethical. Even worse, since neither sale was legal, the entire situation created a convoluted mess that was certain to unravel in the future.

Because of Ahab's desperate situation, multiplied by Shamus' equally disastrous state of affairs, an untenable situation had been created. My sister, Crystal, and her husband, Clyde, believed they would own a beautiful new condominium that was about to be built. It was a lie. Shamus believed he had a right to sell that condominium before the ground was broken, but he didn't. Ahab and Jezzy believed they had a right to resell the condo to Crystal and Clyde, but they didn't for the same reason Shamus didn't. Even worse, everybody involved, other than Shamus, was family. I was clueless about everything that happened. Nevertheless, without my knowledge or my consent, I was smack dab in the middle of an explosive mess.

Despite my naïveté in this matter, I remember thinking about the future and each of the blessings that would come from the prudent investment I had made in Pelican Gulf. In fact, I even remember saying to myself—almost prayerfully—"This is really working out for me. What could possibly go wrong?"

Chapter 12

The Truth Always Presents Itself

W hen developers strike a deal, like the one we had made for Pelican Gulf, LLC, the company formed was intended for a short-term venture. It was created for that specific deal only and nothing more. We bought the raw land and built eighty-four condominiums in an area predicted to grow rapidly.

Being as close to Charleston as we were—just over the drawbridge on James Island—retirees wanted to buy our condos. Even yuppies wanted to purchase them. When the construction was nearly complete, with a dozen or so having already been sold, our emphasis changed. We began showing them to prospective buyers much more aggressively and our condos sold quickly.

During this time, I made a pot load of money and should have made a great deal more, but there were two things that prevented me from doing so. One was preventable but the other one was completely unforeseen.

As it turned out, Ahab actually embezzled much more than the original $300,000 from Pelican Gulf. Being the general partner, with the construction company belonging to his son, I never saw the checkbook or accounts payable. I couldn't have written a check, even if I had wanted to. Because they could write checks, this made it easy for Ahab to misappropriate funds. James, my stepbrother, also embezzled money. In addition to the original $300,000 that was embezzled, between the two of them they took an additional $450,000. The embezzled funds came to a total $750,000 in all. These are the funds that I'm sure about, but it could have been a great deal more than that. Because they were very clever in the way they did it, I doubt I'll ever know the exact number. As bad as this was, it wasn't the biggest problem Pelican Gulf had.

In 2006, we finished construction. By 2007, we had sold most of the units, but there were still quite a few that were on the market. Then, the unthinkable happened. The housing market crashed and we felt its devastating impact—particularly on James Island, South Carolina.

Instead of the remaining units selling at a steady rate, like they had been since we completed construction, sales came to a complete standstill. We couldn't give the units away. Just like so many other real estate investments throughout America, our cash flow shriveled to nothing. To make matters worse, many of our buyers, feeling the economic pinch, reneged on their commitments to purchase the condos and wanted their down payments returned.

If things had remained stable, which they didn't, the money embezzled might have been available for Ahab and James to repay the company. Unfortunately, the crash in the housing market didn't make this possible. Ahab's cash cow had stopped producing milk. Since this was his only profitable venture, with his other investments draining away his limited funds, he couldn't even begin to repay his debt to Shamus. Obviously, this created a great deal of tension between them. Although longtime friends, Ahab knew that Shamus was a person he shouldn't cross. Doing so might be a fatal mistake.

By this time, I had become aware that not everything was as it should be. Things were not being done straightforwardly and aboveboard at Pelican Gulf, which made me glad it was a short-term deal. At the end of that year, the purpose for the three-way partnership was complete and the partnership was ready to dissolve. It was at this time that I was alerted to their theft because the money I was expecting returned to me was no longer in the company.

When Ahab and James left the partnership I had no other choice but to remain onboard *Pelican Gulf, LLC*. There were many reasons I kept the LLC. I knew that by staying in the partnership I was becoming deeply enmeshed in their mess rather than extricating myself from it. Everything I did deepened my involvement in this fiasco and I began to wonder if I would ever be free from it. But there were responsibilities I could not shy away from and I decided to do the right thing and take care of them.

Hester had taken my children, my money and my good name. Now, five years later, her father and her brother had also wounded me and stole a substantial amount of money from me. That they were capable of such a massive deception surprised me, but not as much as you might think. I should have known something like this would happen. I should never have gotten involved with them, but I did. After all, my dad warned me about Ahab the day I married his conniving daughter.

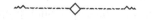

Meanwhile, Shamus was relentless in his efforts to collect his one million dollars from Ahab. Being hounded by someone like Shamus put a great deal of pressure on my stepfather and my mother. Although Ahab and Shamus had been doing business for years and were friends of a sort, because so much money was involved, my stepfather knew Shamus was reaching his breaking point.

In an effort to calm the troubled waters, Ahab agreed to re-title unit 1066 to Shamus as a means of repaying some of the money he owed. The unit certainly wasn't worth the full amount of the loan. It wasn't even close to being valued at what we had assumed it would be by that time. Certainly, the Housing market crash at that time didn't help, but it was all Ahab had to offer at the time. Although it didn't appease Shamus, it was something and it did take the pressure off for a while. Throughout all of this, I had never been informed about this deal. Like everything else between the two of them, the deal was made under the table.

When my two-year stint of being a landlord was complete, I began selling the remaining units in the development to recoup the money Ahab and my stepbrother had stolen from me. This included unit 1066. When the partnership dissolved, unit 1066 was left in the Pelican Gulf partnership where it was born. The deed never moved, despite the back-and-forth dealings between Ahab and Shamus. What they had done between them was an unrecorded deal that was neither legal nor contractually enforceable.

I was now the sole owner of Pelican Gulf, and unit 1066 was left behind as part of the corporation. This meant it belonged to me. It was completely mine along with many other units that were not sold. Selling each of them would help me regain most of the funds Ahab and his son had stolen from me, but not all of it.

When I did sell 1066, which I had every right to do, Ahab and my mother became furious. They demanded that I return it to them, claiming it was their personal property. As brazen as they were, they were actually offended when I wouldn't deed the property back to them. They claimed that I had stolen it from them. As financially destitute as they were, this is how out of touch with reality they had become. I was not only flabbergasted by their effrontery and false accusations, I was pissed. Ahab and his son had stolen at least $750,000 from the company, which meant they had stolen it from me, but that wasn't enough. Like a good boy, Ahab expected me to play ball with him and return the unit, but I refused. I didn't even consider it.

I was tired of getting ripped off by the Dimesdales and I told my stepfather exactly that. When I did, this rubbed my mother and him the wrong way. They couldn't believe that I would do something as unethical and underhanded as keep unit 1066, which belonged to them because they had purchased it from Shamus. In their minds, engaging in revisionist history, by twisting the truth, they became the victims and I became the thief.

Their perverted perspective was ridiculous and I told them so. I had had it with their conniving ways and would never allow myself to be fooled by them again. To me, hearing them rant and whine about their situation reminded me of a woman who murdered her husband and then threw herself on the mercy of the court, bemoaning the fact that she was a widow.

I was done with their self-serving nonsense. My days of being subservient to Ahab and my mother were finished. Although my financial situation wasn't nearly as desperate as theirs, everything I had done was on the up-and-up. Nothing my stepfather had done was ethical, straightforward or honest. From day one, his plan had been to use me, abuse me in our partnership and eventually discard me after having wrung the last dollar out of me. Finally accepting this as the true report, I never wanted to have anything to do with him again. That Ahab was married to my mother and was my children's grandfather made my decision a difficult one to execute, but I was determined to stay away from the Dimesdales for the rest of my life.

I was no longer willing to live in a house just down the street from them, so I sold my home in Greer, South Carolina and moved to West Palm Beach, Florida. After becoming situated, I began working for my brother, Rodney. Through thick and thin, like a big brother should be, Rodney was always there for me. I will never forget what he has done for me, not even if I live to be a hundred years old.

Although I was unwilling to give unit 1066 to Ahab, he certainly wasn't willing to accept my decision. He wouldn't allow himself to be "wronged" like that. Incensed that I wouldn't return "his property," while refusing to address the issue of his massive embezzlement, he and my mother drove to Charleston to see Pelican Gulf's corporate lawyer. They intended to use our lawyer to force me to return "their condo" to them.

When the two of them met with Duffy Tipton, they told him the whole story about how Ahab had bought the property from Shamus with a handshake. Demanding that the deed for condo 1066 be transferred to them based upon that contractual agreement, they wanted Duffy to make their illegal transaction legal. This was something Duffy was unwilling to do knowing he might lose his license to practice law for participating in something illegal. Despite their attempts to bully Duffy into creating false documentation, Pelican Gulf's lawyer wouldn't have anything to do with perpetrating a fraud. That Ahab and Jezzy would demand such a thing indicates just how desperate they had become.

After arguing back and forth for nearly an hour, Duffy demanded that they leave his office. With no alternative and recognizing that they were getting nowhere with the lawyer, they reluctantly left. Fully convinced that they were the victims in the matter, they remained furious.

Having just heard their vitriol and bitter resentment about what had happened, coupled with seeing the malice written on their faces, Duffy became concerned for my personal safety. He contacted me the minute they left his office. He was a little scared for his own safety too. Additionally, since he remained counsel for Pelican Gulf, he had an obligation to inform me about the meeting that had just transpired.

Being the sole owner of Pelican Gulf, he wanted to inform me of everything that had just transpired behind my back. As I listened to what he said, almost none of which I had known before, I was flabbergasted. Nevertheless, once he began to explain things, the pieces to the puzzle finally began to fall into place. His explanation was so enlightening that I didn't even resent paying the bill for his time—not much anyway.

When the conversation ended, I was shaking. Some of it was from trepidation but most of it was from rage. I had finally come to the point where I was willing to admit to myself that my own mother was part of the plot to destroy me financially. She had never been on my side. The thought of such treachery made my stomach lurch and I nearly vomited. I felt exactly the way I did when I was ten—a little boy about to be given away by my mother who didn't love me. That was the day when she packed my bag and wanted to put me up for adoption.

This time she had been able to follow through with her threat to abandon me. Obviously, this realization was difficult for me to internalize and accept. I needed to because it was the truth.

I wish this had been the end of it, but it wasn't. Although Ahab and Jezzy had failed in their attempt to have "their condo" re-titled to them, they were still on the hook to Shamus for one million dollars. To make matters worse for them, he was relentless in pressuring them for payment. He called them daily, like a collection agent for a loan shark. Ahab most likely blurted out, "We don't have the money. Take it up with Steve. He has all the money. We don't have anything."

Doing his best to make his problem mine, Ahab told Shamus that I had the deed to unit 1066. Not yet finished throwing me under the bus, Ahab concluded, "If you want your money back, you'll have to get it from Steve."

Shamus, who was used to following Ahab's directions, since he had been doing deals with him for decades, internalized what Ahab was saying. He also read between the lines of what Ahab wasn't saying. Shamus heard the message loud and clear.

Turning his interest from Ahab and my mother, knowing the well was dry where they were concerned, he refocused his attention on me. If they couldn't pay him his one million dollar, he intended to get it from me.

Like everything else concerning my investment with Pelican Gulf, I had no idea any of this had transpired. I just wanted to liquidate the remaining condos, re-coup my losses as much as possible and go on with my life. Shamus stopped me dead in my tracks.

Ahab and Jezzy wanted to keep me from selling unit 1066, but they couldn't. I had already sold the unit and it was about to close without a problem. It infuriated all of them.

Without my knowledge, Shamus put a lien on the remaining units. Since he had no financial involvement with any of them, there was no legitimate reason for him to do so, but he did it anyway.

With liens put on all condos I was in the process of selling, the transactions were stopped. The only thing left for me to do was have the liens lifted in order to sell the properties. I was dead in the water.

Chapter 13

Another Twist
In The Story

I can't begin to express how relieved I was when unit 1066 was sold. It had been an albatross around my neck for such a long time. Because Ahab and my mother had been so contentious about its disposition, all I wanted to do was get rid of the condo. When I closed on the property, I jumped for joy because I thought all the trouble with Ahab and Jezzy was behind me.

As I was in the process of selling the second unit, I was surprised to find that a lien had been put on it. I discovered there were liens on the other unsold condos as well. This meant I couldn't sell any of them. When I learned that Shamus O'Dunnigan had been the person who secured the liens on the condos, I was even more surprised.

Since he didn't have a financial interest in any of them and I didn't owe him any money—not a dime—I couldn't imagine why he had done such a thing. Nevertheless, his actions definitely made me furious.

Despite my vexation, I had no choice other than to contact Shamus and find a way to have the liens removed. Although dreading a confrontation I picked up the phone and called Shamus.

After saying hello, exchanging pleasantries and asking him how he was, which I didn't care about, I came straight to the point for my call. "Shamus," I said, "When I sold unit C-105, I was informed that a lien had been placed on the property and it was done by you."

"What?" Shamus replied, clearly surprised and genuinely mystified by how such a thing could have happened.

"You know I can't sell the condo until you remove that lien, right?" I added, rhetorically. "In fact, I can't sell any of them, since you put liens on all of the remaining condos. I can't close on any of them."

"Steve, I can't imagine how such a thing could have happened," Shamus replied apologetically. "There must have been some kind of mistake. I can't conceive of how this occurred?"

I didn't believe him, of course, but that didn't matter. I still had to deal with the problem.

"Well, it happened," I stated, "and I'm dead in the water until your lien is removed." In replying to him, I laughed a little—just to keep things from becoming contentious. The last thing I needed was a battle with Shamus O'Dunnigan.

Shamus laughed as well, but his mirth was just as disingenuous as mine. A moment later, he said, "I don't want to hold you up, Steve. I know you need to get your money back."

"I sure do," I concurred. "I definitely need to sell the units."

Knowing what kind of bind I was in, Shamus came up with a solution. "Why don't you take a drive up here and meet me at my house?" He added, "That way, I can sign the papers and remove the lien. You remember where my house is in Mount Pleasant, don't you?"

"I'm not sure I've ever been to your house," I replied, "but I can put your address in my GPS. No problem," I added.

"I know it's a long drive from West Palm, but why don't you come up on Thursday? Let's say about noon."

"I can come up, but there is no way I can make it that early. It's a 500-mile drive," I reminded him.

"Oh, I didn't know it was that far. When I go down there, I always fly," Shamus replied. He seemed to be surprised by how far it actually was. "How about 6 p.m. then? That will give you enough time to get here, won't it?"

"Yes, I think I can make it by then. That will work. I'll see you at your house on Thursday at 6 p.m." I added, verifying the day and the hour I intended to meet him.

"See you then, Steve," Shamus said amiably. "I'm looking forward to it," he added, disconnecting a moment later.

As you can imagine, I didn't want to drive all the way up I-95 to Charleston, which was at least a seven-hour trip, but I had no choice in the matter. Until the liens on the condos were removed, he was in the diver's seat. I wasn't. Instead, I had become his economic hostage.

Besides, I didn't have any confidence in sending all the documents that needed to be signed and witnessed via FedEx. I needed to make sure everything was done correctly and each document was handled appropriately. To move forward and sell the remaining condos, which would allow me to regain nearly all of what I had lost, everything needed to be done to meet the exacting specifications of the closing attorney. That being the case, I knew I needed to take care of things myself. There was no other alternative.

One good thing that was going for me at the time was having my youngest son Daniel visiting for the summer. He lived with his mom in Washington State so I didn't get to see him very often. I cherished every moment we were together so I decided to take him along with me for the ride.

By taking him with me to Charleston, I decided to make the entire trip an adventure. It would be fun and make the long drive less grueling. With just the two of us in the car, we would be able to talk for hours. Besides, since it was a straight shot up

I-95, we would see some incredible scenery and I would be able to point out some interesting landmarks about American history along the way. When I thought of the trip in those terms, instead of it being a thankless ordeal, I actually looked forward to going.

That's also how I sold the idea to Daniel. The trip to Charleston would also allow me to pick up a check for the sale of the condo. Having that money in my pocket would help out a lot. Thinking about it like this, I became enthusiastic about our journey.

⸻◇⸻

The evening before we left, I went through all of my papers again. I wanted to make sure each of the lien release forms was in order. Although it was infuriating to have to go through this hoop just to sell a piece of property Shamus had nothing to do with, I calmed my nerves as much as possible. I also knew that if I stayed mad during the long drive up, it would have spoiled my time with my twelve-year-old. I definitely didn't want to do that.

To add to our adventure, we drove my BMW M-5, which had a 500-horsepower engine. Although Daniel didn't like the idea that I had to work during his vacation, he loved going places in the BMW. To make the adventure more palatable for both of us, I booked a nice room at a decent hotel where we also planned to spend the weekend. It would allow us to take in some of the sights in Charleston, which is one of the most charming cities in the country. I especially wanted to point out the numerous Civil War monuments that could be found throughout the city.

From my perspective, the thing that interested me the most about Charleston was its fine restaurants. While we were there, I intended to eat low country barbeque at least twice. It's different than any other kind and, in my opinion, the best. I especially like the ribs. Some people don't like the vinegary taste but I don't mind it one bit.

We set out at 8:30 a.m., which was half an hour later than I planned. I didn't factor getting a twelve-year-old out of bed and into gear, especially during his summer vacation, as a possible delay. Once we were in the car and headed north, I tried to engage Daniel in conversation numerous times. Being the twelve-year-old boy that he was, he was far more interested in his Game Boy than anything else.

We passed many beautiful sights that I made sure to point out but he would simply look up for a second, nod his head and then return to his video game. This was frustrating and a little irritating. Struggling to make a connection, I didn't say anything about it. I had hoped he would keep me better company on the long drive than he did, but I was glad to have him with me anyway. If I made the trip by myself it would have been much more grueling.

When we arrived in Charleston, I pointed out some of the beautiful old homes to him and he paid better attention. Because we started out later than I had anticipated, making several stops along the way, we didn't have time to check into our hotel before meeting Shamus at his house.

I didn't want to be a minute late. I didn't want to give the old curmudgeon any excuse to not sign the papers. Since I was at his mercy until they were signed, I planned to be completely professional with him about everything. Just to make sure things were set for our meeting, I called Shamus earlier in the afternoon when Daniel and I had just driven past Saint Simon's Island, in Georgia. Shamus answered promptly and said he would be there to meet me—no problem.

Believing I had done everything correctly to ensure that the meeting would go smoothly, while also being as brief as possible, I highlighted the places where Shamus needed to sign the papers before I left West Palm Beach. I didn't want to leave anything to chance knowing how important getting the papers signed was.

If everything went as smoothly as I hoped they would, the meeting could be as short as five minutes—maybe even shorter than that. I realized this was my best-case scenario and what I prayed would happen. To facilitate this, I went to considerable trouble to achieve my goal.

The only deviation I made to my original plan was taking Daniel with me to Shamus' house. I didn't know whether or not Shamus had children, but I felt sure he would understand my situation, especially since we had just arrived from such a long, grueling trip.

Although I was somewhat familiar with Charleston, I didn't know the streets well enough to go to Shamus' house without the aid of my GPS. As we neared his house, I was impressed by his neighborhood. It was beautiful. Each house had its own unique design. No two were alike and each was immaculately landscaped. Being in construction, I always appreciated great architecture. Driving through his neighborhood, it seemed like each home had a luxury automobile or sports car parked in the driveway. He lived in the "old money" part of town.

Needless to say, I was impressed by his surroundings. Just like my stepfather and mother, Shamus lived the good life. Finally arriving at his house, I pulled into his driveway. Placing the car in neutral, I engaged the parking brake and left the engine running. As hot as it was outside on a June afternoon in the Deep South, I wanted to keep the air conditioning running for Daniel's sake.

Turning to him as I unbuckled my seatbelt, I said, "This will only take a couple of minutes. You can just wait in the car, if that's what you want."

"Okay, Dad," Daniel replied, completely immersed in his Game Boy. Now that I think about it, I don't believe he even looked up at me when he replied.

The heat was oppressive as I got out of the car. The decision to leave the air conditioning on in the car was definitely the right choice. Taking a deep breath, I walked up the stairs to Shamus O'Dunnigan's front door, knocked and then rang his bell.

While I waited for him to come to the door, I looked back at my son who was still engrossed in his video game. He looked so cute. Being my last child, like other parents, I wished that he would never grow up. I wanted him to remain just the way he was—Game Boy and all.

While standing there, I studied the large pillars on the front of the house. Having built homes for so long, I appreciated the fine construction of Shamus' house. Since he hadn't responded, I rang the doorbell again. He still didn't answer, which seemed odd to me. I had been very clear about the time of my arrival and both of us agreed to it.

Although Daniel was waiting in the car, I could tell he was getting impatient. I know I was. After ringing and knocking a third time and still receiving no answer, I called Shamus. It went immediately to his voicemail. I waited a few minutes on the porch, sweating profusely because of the hot afternoon sun and called a second time. This call went straight to his voicemail again.

Having waited at least fifteen minutes fruitlessly and with no other choice, I finally gave up. Walking back to the car, I was not only disappointed, I was also irritated. It was infuriating to have come so far only to be stood up by my stepfather's buddy. I was incensed. Even worse, I had no choice other than to be accommodating. I knew it would be impossible to sell the condo without getting Shamus to release the liens. He knew this too, of course, and I suspected he was just making it difficult for me— probably just to be spiteful.

When I returned to the car, Daniel asked, "Did you get the papers signed, Dad?"

Looking at him sitting there, in spite of being as angry as I was, I had to smile. Daniel was so cute. He had been so engrossed in his video game that he didn't even look up at me—

not once. If he had, he would have seen me standing there by myself like a fool in the hot afternoon sun.

Answering his question, I said, "No, Shamus wasn't home. Maybe we can try again later."

Having been unsuccessful and still in possession of the unsigned papers, I drove to the Hilton Garden Inn. It was near the airport and about a twenty-minute drive from Shamus' house. After checking in, we brought our suitcases to our room and began to settle in. While Daniel was hooking up his game system to the TV, I tried to call Shamus again. There was still no answer. By that time I was no longer mad. I had become nervous because I needed to get the papers signed.

About an hour later, much to my relief, Shamus called me back. He invited me to return to his house saying that he had just arrived at the airport having flown in from Florida.

I thought this was a little odd. Earlier in the day he told me he was in town and at his house. Obviously, something didn't jive and it was unsettling. This should have been a huge red flag, but my need to get him to sign the releases trumped my need to be cautious with Shamus.

Changing the subject, sensing accurately that I was a little agitated, he talked about some other insignificant thing for a while. I can't even remember what it was. When he recognized I had settled down a bit, he invited me to return to his house at 9:00 p.m., assuring me that he would sign the papers then. After agreeing to meet him, since it was already 8:40 p.m., I grabbed my keys and wallet. In less than a minute I was ready to head out the door.

"We need to go back to Shamus' house, Daniel," I told my son, "He's there now, so we've got to go."

"I don't want to go Dad," Daniel whined. "It's my summer vacation. Just let me stay here, please?" Now pleading, he added, "I won't be able to do anything while you're there. Besides, you'll end up visiting with him for hours."

Although I had no intention of staying to talk to Shamus once I got the papers signed, my son was right. He would be better off staying in the room by himself with the door locked rather than driving over to Shamus' with me. Besides, he had finally succeeded in getting his game system to work on the TV and he was very excited to try out the new game I had just bought him.

Nevertheless, I felt uncomfortable about leaving Daniel alone at the hotel. Although he was old enough to be on his own for short periods, I still didn't like the idea. No father would. He kept telling me I was being overprotective. Perhaps he was right, I mused. As so often happens with kids his age, his persistence got the better of me. Before I left, I made him solemnly promise to not leave the room. I also made him promise to keep the door locked. Having my own key, I made him commit to not opening the door for anyone—not for any reason.

Once he promised, crossing his heart, I headed out the door to Shamus' house. Come hell or high water, I was ready to get the papers signed. I not only needed the money, but I also felt compelled to get these people out of my life. During my short drive over to his house, I felt strong and purposeful. I was also apprehensive. I'm not sure why I had a terrible sense of foreboding.

Chapter 14

Bad Business

s I passed over the bridge from Charleston, connecting it to Mount Pleasant and several of the islands, I was deep in thought. Traveling its expanse provided a breathtaking view I always loved. This trip across was different—I was so engrossed in my thoughts I didn't even consider the beauty of my surroundings. I couldn't. My focus had to be entirely on the purpose for my trip.

By this point in my dealings with my mother and my stepfather, I knew I couldn't trust either of them with anything. I wouldn't even consider it. They had demonstrated in spades how duplicitous and dishonest they could be. As bad as they had been, they continued to front that they were paragons of virtue. I suppose they were when compared to Shamus O'Dunnigan.

He was a true reprobate. Having heard stories about his nefarious shenanigans for years, I felt a little nervous about meeting him. Nevertheless, I did the best I could to dismiss my trepidation. I needed to remain calm.

Besides, Shamus may have been a mean hombre years ago but he was a seventy-year-old man now. How tough could he be? Being his junior by nearly a quarter of a century, I felt a little foolish worrying about having a physical altercation with him. Regardless of how confrontational our meeting might become,

I couldn't imagine Shamus beating me up. Besides, if worse came to worst, I felt certain I could take him on.

Pulling into his driveway, I decided my best strategy was to stay out of his house. All I needed was his signature in several places, which could easily be taken care of on the front porch. That left our business dealing out in the open for all his neighbors to see. Looking at my watch, I congratulated myself for arriving at Shamus house promptly at 9 p.m., just as I had committed to do when he called less than a half hour earlier. To make sure I wasn't late, I had driven fast, which wasn't a problem in a BMW M5.

Once again, I stood at his front door, knocked, waited and received no answer. This was beyond exasperating. It was so infuriating that I had to fight my emotions just to keep from getting angry. He had jerked me around enough.

I tried knocking a second time and received no answer again. Annoyed and beginning to wonder if I had wasted my time by making the trip, I decided to call him.

"Hello?" He answered immediately.

"Shamus, this is Steve. I'm here at your house. I've knocked twice and you haven't answered."

Surprised to hear this, Shamus said apologetically, "Oh I'm so sorry Steve. I guess I didn't hear you. Just come on inside, the door isn't locked."

Not feeling comfortable intruding like that, I replied, "That's alright. I'll just wait here until you can come to the door."

Understanding how I felt, Shamus said he would be right there and disconnected. He didn't come to the door right away though. In all honesty, it felt like he was being passive-aggressive. Having been married to a Dimesdale for twenty years, it was a familiar feeling.

As I stood there looking like a fool, I had to wait for Shamus for several more minutes. Finally, he arrived, opened the door with a smile and said, "Come in, Steve. Let's have a drink and talk business."

That's not what I wanted to do, but I didn't think it would be wise to refuse his hospitality. Acting against my better judgment and throwing all caution to the wind, I walked in.

His home was beautiful. It was magnificently appointed and what I liked best was how low he kept his air conditioning. Having been very hot waiting for him on his front porch, it was great to feel the cool air inside. I also noticed a very strong smell of alcohol permeating his house. Later on, I realized it was coming from him. It was quite obvious he had been drinking a lot. Nevertheless, his alcohol consumption didn't seem to impair him in the least. He didn't stumble around, have slurred speech or anything like that. If he was an alcoholic, he was a very controlled one. But I was about to find out that wasn't the case.

Since I had only met him briefly a couple of times before, I looked at him critically, which was something I had never done before. He had a rough look to him but he carried himself confidently. You could tell he liked to be in charge. His hair was completely grey and full, which made him look a little younger than he actually was. Being seventy, as you might expect, his face was worn and wrinkled. His entire countenance exuded the proud, defiant look of a man who had once been very formidable. I had no trouble seeing how people were intimidated by him—especially in his younger years.

Turning to me, Shamus asked pleasantly, "Is your son waiting for you in the car?"

"No, I left Daniel at the hotel." I added, "He's engrossed playing his Game Boy on the TV." A moment later, I stated, "I can't stay long. I've got to get back to him." Addressing my reason for making the trip, I added, "All I need is your signature to get the liens released on the condos."

Taking a pull from the drink he had in his hand while gazing at me in a slightly intimidating way, Shamus finally nodded his head. "Come with me. Let's sit down for a minute. We need to talk. Then I'll sign the releases."

I certainly didn't want to do that so I said, "I really don't have time to do that, Shamus. I need to get back to the hotel. My son is waiting for me. He's only twelve."

"If you want the releases, we need to talk. That's just the way it is." When Shamus said this, he drew a hard line between us—one we both understood was there.

Just as I had feared, obtaining my releases wasn't going to be easy. He fully intended to be contentious. Realizing I couldn't sell the condos without first dealing with him, I knew that it was in my best interest to be accommodating.

"Okay, you win," I said with a forced smile, "but I can't stay long."

He led me from the foyer into the dining room. While walking two steps behind him, I noticed how nice his shoes were. Why this made such an impression on me, I don't know, but it did. I also noticed that they matched his shirt nicely. It was tasteful—not flashy. His entire outfit seemed very well coordinated. It suggested to me that he was more a successful businessman than a gangster. This made me feel better about our meeting.

Taking my seat at the dining room table while Shamus took his seat at the head of it, I saw a folder filled with papers that had been placed right beside him. Acting like we were about to engage in extended negotiations rather than simply signing the forms to release the liens, he began our meeting by opening the folder of papers.

In a very professional way, reminiscent of the way a banker would transact business, he handed me the papers. Catching my eye, Shamus said, "Take a look at these, Steve."

Seeing how thick the stack of papers was, I fretted that I was going to be sitting there for a long time. Obtaining my releases wasn't going to be an easy task. Frankly, I began to suspect that it wasn't even going to happen.

However, I obliged him knowing I had no other choice if the discussion was to proceed. Taking a look through the papers,

I realized Shamus had nearly all of the financial records for my partnership with my stepfather and stepbrother at Pelican Gulf. Having gone through them many times, trying to determine how much had been stolen from the company by my nefarious relatives, I recognized each of the documents quickly and easily. Shuffling through them, I wondered how Shamus got a hold of them. They certainly weren't public records. My guess was Ahab had given them to him. This made me wonder why he would do such a thing? What possible motivation could he have?

While these questions swirled around my head, Shamus interrupted my pondering.

In a slightly intimidating way, he demanded, "How much money did you make from the condo project, Steve?"

Placing the folder back on the table, I stared at him. Although it was none of his business how much I made, I decided to answer his question. Looking him straight in the eye, I replied honestly, "None. I haven't broken even yet. I'm actually owed money from this deal."

Because my answer didn't sit well with Shamus, his mannerisms changed. He became agitated, but calmed himself quickly and was able to maintain his control. To settle down or perhaps embolden himself, he took a long pull from his glass of whiskey.

Seeing this, I hoped it wasn't alcohol that was controlling him. My concern, which had been moderate, increased substantially knowing that nothing good ever comes from arguing with a drunk.

Leaning forward in an obvious attempt to intimidate me, Shamus pressed his finger into the table—just like he would have done to my chest, if he had been close enough to do it. I was glad I hadn't given him the opportunity by leaning forward.

"Ahab owes me a lot of money," Shamus snarled. "I need to be paid before I will sign your releases."

The cards were on the table now. Shamus had played his hand and it was clear I wasn't going to get my papers signed.

I had driven 500 miles on a fool's errand. Everything had become abundantly clear to me: My stepfather and mother had convinced Shamus that I would pay their debt back because I still had some money.

Nevertheless, I knew it was not in my best interest to match his aggressiveness. Trying to reason with him, I said, "My stepdad owes me a lot of money too. This project wrecked my relationship with him and my mother." Continuing, I added, "I have even considered filing a lawsuit against Ahab for fraud and embezzlement but figured it wasn't worth the ..."

Interrupting me before I could finish my sentence, Shamus abandoned any pretense of civility. Taking the gloves off, he yelled, "Listen to me, you piece of shit!"

When he said this, I knew our meeting was going to end badly.

Intent on intimidating me, Shamus raised his voice. Practically shouting, although I was only two feet away from him, he snapped: "I know you cashed in on this condo project. I'm owed a lot of fucking money and you had better pay up."

Being very calm and making sure to measure my words, I replied. "No. I'm not going to pay you anything. Why should I? I don't owe you any money."

Hearing my response and recognizing the resolve I had in my voice, Shamus flew into a rage. He became quite animated. Standing while I remained seated, he knocked over his drink, which spilled onto the floor. Unconcerned about the whiskey staining his marble, his arms flailed while his fists became clenched.

Turning his head and looking out the window, he screamed. "Do I need to start fucking killing people?"

A moment later, returning his gaze to me, he said. "Ahab owes me one million dollars, damn it!"

Once he lost control and his rage intensified, Shamus could no longer contain himself. He strung together a litany of profanity worthy of a sailor. Cursing God, Ahab and me in a way I never could have imagined, he continued to work himself up. I suppose he thought this would scare me into complying with his repeated demand for money. It actually had the exact opposite effect on me.

Although cornered, I knew the time to remain calm and compliant had passed. Matching his intensity, I shouted back at him. "I don't owe you anything! Ahab owes you—not me!"

This got his attention. Looking me straight in the eye, getting so close to me I could smell the liquor on his foul breath, he said, "I'm going to kill you right now if you don't fix this."

There it was. His intimidation had become life threatening. Having just threatened to murder me, I knew I needed to stand my ground.

"Don't bully me," I replied, sneering contemptuously at this seventy-year-old has-been. "Your threats won't work on me. You don't know who you're dealing with do you? I'm Steve Sarkela!"

Waiting for that to sink in, I stood and assumed a defensive position. Ready to fight. I added, "You can't just bring me in here and push me around. I've had enough of you. This isn't worth getting the lien released."

Knowing I could take this old man, if push came to shove, I also knew that it would be unwise to hit him. Instead, I simply turned my back and started to leave.

When I did, Shamus yelled, "Otto!"

When he said this, when he summoned another person, my heart froze. I heard footsteps coming towards us from another room and they were moving very fast. At that precise instant, I knew I was in a world of trouble. Turning to Shamus, our eyes locked and I saw him for who he was. I had heard that he was a killer and now I knew for sure that he was. I could see it in his cold, merciless and dead eyes.

Chapter 15

Fighting to Live

T he moment Shamus called for Otto—a person who carefully concealed himself in another room—my life changed irreversibly. It has never been the same since and never will be. Shamus and Otto's lives changed too. Maybe even more so than my own.

When I heard Otto's footsteps racing toward me, I didn't have time to think about the long-term implications of what was about to happen. I didn't even have the luxury of being philosophical about it. Intuitively, I knew my life was in danger. And I was scared. This made me incapable of thinking clearly. Being in stark terror immobilized me and I wasn't able to react— the precise thing I needed to do. As panic gripped my stomach, heart and throat, I became irresolute and remained stationary for what seemed like an eternity.

Time seemed to slow down to a standstill, but the pace of Otto's footsteps didn't. As my heart continued to pound in my chest, the sound from it matched the cadence of Otto's footsteps. Instantly, my mouth became dry and I knew my life hung in the balance.

Recognizing the footsteps were coming from my left, I turned my head to see who was approaching. That's when Otto's fist, coming out of the shadows like a demonic apparition, hit me so hard on the side of my head that my knees buckled. Dazed and disoriented, I fell to the floor. Time felt like it had stopped when his fist made impact with my face. Disoriented from the force of Otto's crushing punch, I didn't know where I was. I wasn't sure whether or not what was happening was real. Being as stunned as I was, I thought I might be dreaming.In the blink of an eye, the bleak reality came crashing down on me—just as suddenly as Otto's fist had. That's when I became certain my life was in peril.

Before I could regain my footing, my attacker continued his assault and beat me to the floor. He was merciless. He just kept hitting, kicking and pummeling me back down to the ground. Despite the relentlessness of his attack, knowing my life was in jeopardy, I kept trying to regain my footing. Finally managing to do so, one of Otto's punches connected solidly with the left side of my ribs and I winced from the pain. This was followed by a kick to my lower back almost immediately. Otto was a skilled fighter.

Using the momentum of the kick, which hurt like hell, I managed to roll over and finally scrambled to my feet. When I did, I got a good look at my attacker. He was in his twenties, six-feet tall, blonde, trim and very fit. Angular, with sinewy muscles, he had a square jaw and large forehead.

A moment later, he hit me solidly in the stomach. The hit temporarily sent me back down to the floor. I couldn't breathe from the force of the blow, which made me panic. Making things worse, my attacker was relentless. He didn't stop—not once. There was no respite from his persistent assault. I was struggling just to get air in my lungs. It seemed like he was hell bent on killing me.

Time after time, his punches hit me in the ribs. They weren't light punches either. I could feel the force of them going straight through me—right to the bone—cracking them. Otto hit me like Rocky Balboa hit the side of beef in the meat locker. To protect my ribs, I rolled over onto my stomach, but that only made matters worse. Instead of hitting me in the ribs, Otto's punches hit my kidneys. These blows were even more painful. They sent shooting pain throughout my body He was like a shark going wild at the smell of blood. Seeing me in so much pain only seemed to fuel his vicious attack.

With blood running down my forehead and dripping into my eyes from his initial punch, I did my best to assume a fetal position. I did this in an effort to protect my face. He slammed the side of my head with his fist when I moved defensively to protect my eyes. At the same time, he kicked me in the groin. The blow to my head reverberated in my ears but that wasn't the worst part. He kicked me in the balls forcing me to recoil in pain.

While I was writhing in agony, Otto used my vulnerability to place me in a chokehold. He fully intended to cut off my breathing, which would render me unconscious and possibly end my life.As brutal and relentless as my assault had been so far, despite everything, Otto had not defeated me. I was not yet finished. In fact, I had just begun to fight.

With his forearm around my throat, I knew that if I lost consciousness from his chokehold, I might not survive. Using strength and resolve I didn't know I possessed, I fought my way off the ground and back to my feet. By standing up straight, I was able to lift him up as well. Once up, I moved his arm over my head and broke the chokehold he had on me.

Now, with both of us on our feet and standing a couple of feet apart, we looked at each other menacingly. Having broken his death grip and simultaneously regaining my balance, I was once again able to breathe. Feeling adrenaline rush through my body, I became strengthened for our next round of conflict.

Seeing Otto's look of astonishment, which I think came from being surprised that I still had any fight left in me, I felt good about myself for the first time since he had entered the room. Honestly, I was equally astonished at the fact that I was standing again. I had no other choice than to put up a vigorous defense because I was fighting for my life. I mustered every fiber of resolve remaining in my body to stay alive and fight to make it out of there.

Although I had taken quite a beating, Otto had expended quite a bit of energy. By throwing as many punches as he had, he was not nearly as fresh as he had been when his assault began. As we stood there for a brief second appraising one another and with Shamus cheering on his champion, I could see that Otto was breathing hard. This meant that he was not nearly as formidable as he had been just a few minutes earlier. At least this was my assumption.

Seizing my opportunity, I made a break for the front door knowing that if I could get outside where the neighbors could see a struggle ensuing, someone would undoubtedly call the police. While running, I tried to pull my phone out of my pocket and dial 911, but I was moving too fast to hit the numbers correctly. Instead of 911, I dialed 711 and then 811. Meanwhile, I continued to move toward the door with Otto doing his best to block me with his punches and kicks.

Unable to dial 911 correctly, Otto successfully kicked the phone out of my hand and it fell to the floor. My phone fell and I could see the battery fly out. Watching this for a split second, I took my eyes off of Otto. It was a big mistake and it cost me.

Seizing his opportunity, Otto kicked me squarely in the chest. The blow was so hard I fell back on a table, crashing to the floor a moment later. The force of the kick was devastating. Lying flat on my back, I was at Otto's mercy once again, which was disheartening. To stay alive I knew I had to get back up and somehow get out of Shamus' house. If I didn't, I would die right then and there. I was sure of it.

Delighted that he had assumed the upper hand once again, Otto kicked me repeatedly. His goal was to incapacitate me completely. It felt like it was working as I lay there on the floor. I started to lose energy and I nearly lost consciousness. Although

I felt faint and weak, nearly abandoning my resolve to continue resisting, but at the deepest level of my being I couldn't find it in myself to quit. My will to live was strong and it definitely motivated me to fight back.

After one particularly punishing kick, everything seemed like it was a dream to me again. Time had once again slowed down and I was no longer capable of mustering an adequate defense. Nevertheless, I wasn't finished. Despite the repeated blows I was receiving, I began to crawl towards the front door. Getting outside was my only chance to live. One of Otto's kicks missed, which made him lose his balance and he fell to the floor. While he was down, which I knew wouldn't be for long, I managed to get back up on my feet. Once up, although woozy, I bolted for the door.

Terrified that I would reach the door, open it and get outside, Shamus cut me off. He was screaming and swearing: "I'm going to kill you, you fucker."

Believing he meant what he said, I pushed past him. When I did, he tackled me around my ankles and I fell to the floor once again. All of this happened in a split second. A moment later, Otto re-entered the fray by jumping on my back while I was trying to regain my footing. He twisted my arms behind my back and pulled them out of my shoulder joints. Feeling my muscles tear from the strain was excruciating.

While all of this was occurring, Shamus released my legs, got to his feet and picked up a broken drinking glass that had fallen from the table. All the while, Otto continued to lock my arms behind my head and increase his pressure. It felt like he was going to completely twist my arms off. As he held me there, Shamus started hitting and beating me. As he did, he howled repeated obscenities at me—not like a human would, but more like a disembodied evil spirit. The malice of his words was more intimidating than his feeble blows.

A minute later, he stopped. With a look of pure hatred, he took the broken glass, placed it an inch from my face and said,

"I'm going to cut your fucking eyes out. Then I'm going to slit your throat."

His threat terrified me, especially since I knew he meant what he said. I could see the cruelty in his inebriated eyes, which were bulging with red-hot hate. His look was one of pure evil. What made it worse was it came from a man who had been my stepfather's business associate for half a century.

Addressing Otto, Shamus said, "Bring him to the chair."

When I heard this, I realized this entire episode had been planned in advance. Even before I came to the house, these villains had meticulously planned my execution. Fearing imminent death, my survival instinct kicked in big time. To bring me to the chair they had waiting, Otto had to release me from his full nelson grip. Once semi-free, when he began dragging me toward the stairs by my arm, I grabbed the doorframe and held onto it for dear life.

Undeterred by my response, Otto yanked on my ankles in an effort to pull me away, but he couldn't break my grip. At one point, he was pulling so hard that my legs were off the ground and actually came close to being parallel with the floor. This is how strenuously he was pulling, but I was equally determined to maintain my grip on the doorframe. I could tell he was getting tired from pulling and also from hitting me so many times, which was very encouraging.

The tables were about to turn in my favor and I could feel it. I knew that if I held on long enough, I might survive. Once Otto's strength was gone and he dropped my legs, which I felt would be very soon, I would be on my feet again and I could get outside. It was my only chance.

Shamus also recognized what was happening and intervened.

"I will kill you right here!" Shamus screamed at me. In an instant, he raced out of the foyer and headed for the kitchen. A moment later, he returned with a large serrated knife, which he brandished in his right hand.

Seeing the knife, my heart sank. I felt certain he was going to use it on me.

Placing the knife to my throat, I felt its pressure on my jugular vein.

Knowing how scared I was, Shamus hissed in my ear. "Let go or I will cut your throat right here."

I believed him. Tired and scared, I released my grip and fell to the floor where I was completely at the mercy of Otto, who was still holding my feet. My life was in their hands now and I doubted I would live through the night.

That's when I started to think of my son. He was alone at the hotel and he was only twelve. Since I hadn't returned, he would start to get worried. As desperate as my situation was, being a dad, Daniel's situation also concerned me. There was nothing I could do for my son.

Chapter 16

Facing Death

The unprovoked attack on me had been brutal. By this time, I must have sustained at least a hundred blows. Maybe even more. Every fiber of my being hurt, especially my head. It didn't stop throbbing. I was unable to take deep breaths because my ribs hurt so badly and I was thirsty. I could barely move because everything hurt.

In portraying my attack, it has been my intention to be very descriptive about precisely what happened. It's important for me to be as accurate as possible because people too often entertain unrealistic ideas about what being assaulted actually entails. Most of these misconceptions are based on movies and television shows they've seen—few of which are realistic. Being assaulted is much different than Hollywood's fantasized version of it. Reality is far more brutal, especially for someone like me, who was not used to being involved in physical altercations like this.

Knowing my life depended on it, I put up a substantial defense. It took Otto quite a while to subdue me, which I think was surprising to him. At least twenty years my junior and in perfect shape, I'm sure he didn't expect I would put up much of a fight. Had it not been for Shamus holding the large, serrated knife next to my throat, ready to slit it open, I may have managed to get outside. If that had happened, my story would have had a different outcome.

Knowing Shamus was prepared to cut my throat, I had no choice other than to capitulate to his demand to stop resisting. By that time, my strength and willingness to continue fighting had depleted substantially anyway. Exhausted and resigned to whatever fate awaited me, I did as Shamus demanded and ceased my resistance.

With a condescending smirk, Shamus removed the knife from my throat. Like a gazelle run down by a cheetah, I knew I was a dead man. I was forced to comply with the demands of my two predators. Once I stopped struggling, both Otto and Shamus breathed a sigh of relief. Neither suspected it would require such an effort to achieve victory, which must have been as equally exhausting for Otto as it had been for me. Without protestation or struggle, I complied with Otto's leading when he pulled my arms behind my back. Now that he was in control, he began walking me up the stairs. Breathing heavily, exhausted from the brawl, and with little energy remaining, we ascended the stairs slowly.

As we continued up the flight of stairs, with Shamus leading the way and Otto following behind me, I had no idea what awaited me. I only knew that whatever was going to happen wasn't going to be pleasant. In my heart, I felt certain they were going to kill me.

Looking up at Shamus, who was walking sideways—never taking his eyes off of me—I became very fearful and begged for my life. "Please don't do this Shamus," I implored. "You win. I'll give you some money—a lot of it. Anything you want—just don't kill me."

Otto stopped halfway up the stairs. Clearly interested in getting money from me, he asked, "How?"

When I saw this, believing he was more interested in robbing me than killing me, I became encouraged. "I can transfer funds into your account from a computer." I suggested.

Almost immediately, it seemed apparent he had dismissed my idea, believing he had already passed the point of no return.

I could see it in his eyes. His look had transformed from being covetous to being murderous—all within the blink of an eye.

Responding to my suggestion of a wire transfer, he snarled, "Shut up!" Looking at Otto, who was below me, Shamus commanded, "Bring him to the chair."

When we reached the top of the staircase, Shamus paused to take a breath. Seeing how badly the old criminal was out of shape amused me a little but knowing how much trouble I was in, it was a fleeting thought.

A short moment later, we started walking down the hall, which was very long. As we moved, it felt like I was having a bad dream—the one where the door at the end of the hall seems like it always remains very far away. I dreaded reaching it, suspecting I would never survive what was behind the door.

While being led down the hall, I noticed an exercise room to the left of me. It was filled with all sorts of machines to keep Shamus as fit as possible. Finally, we arrived at the door at the end of the hallway. Catching my eye with a look of pure malice, like a cat toying with a trapped mouse, Shamus smirked. It was obvious he was enjoying himself and was actually eager to torture me.

A second later, he opened the door and led me into a very dark room. Actually, it wasn't really even a room. It appeared to be more like a small closet that had been built into the attic. It was quite cramped. When I saw what was waiting for me, my legs buckled. Otto had to catch me to keep me from collapsing. I was terrified, which was obvious to both of my assailants. Shamus chuckled at my dread while Otto remained nonplussed. It was like he was devoid of emotions. With dead eyes, a stoic look and a remorseless countenance, he reminded me of Bogs, one of the villains from *Shawshank Redemption*. Like Bogs, Otto was a man who enjoyed inflicting pain on weak and helpless victims.

In the middle of this empty room was a wooden chair with thick armrests. Resembling the electric chair from *The Green*

Mile, it was the only piece of furniture in the room. It was very solid and had been carefully prepared for me. If I had had any doubt my attack had been premeditated, seeing the chair that awaited me dispelled any notion that this assault had been spontaneous.

"Sit down." Shamus demanded—which I did, complying immediately with his command. Handing the knife to Otto, Shamus left but he returned quickly, holding a roll of duct tape, several strips of white cloth and a pair of scissors. Placing my arms on the armrests of the chair, Shamus placed the white cloth on my wrists, holding each piece tight to the chair. It was exactly the way it would have happened if I had been strapped in an electric chair. Without having to be told what to do, Otto taped my arms to the chair, making sure none of the tape attached to my skin. They bound my arms so tightly that I couldn't have pulled them free—not if my life depended on it.

I was their captive, completely immobilized—no question about it. Once Otto finished, Shamus smiled boastfully. In a self-satisfied way, he said, "This isn't the first time I've done this."

Witnessing his animated expression and seeing the gleeful smirk on his face for myself, all of the stories I had heard over the years about Shamus—which included multiple murders, flooded my mind. Dark images about what was going to happen to me made my body quake with foreboding and trepidation. Seeing how terrified I was pleased Shamus. A true sadist, he was enjoying himself. I was certain of it. Witnessing his pleasure, all of which came at my expense, exacerbated my fear exponentially.

Looking at me, with a malicious smile, Shamus said, "The cloth is used to keep the police from finding any DNA evidence." With this statement, I knew they intended to kill me. By binding me the way they had, they just wanted to make it less likely that the authorities could prove they were responsible for my fate. Coming to this conclusion, my heart sank much deeper into despair. Once my hands were bound securely, they proceeded to do the same thing to my legs—cloth first, then the tape to secure me.

With a smile that displayed how pleased he was with himself, Shamus said, "Please don't think this is for your comfort, Steve. It isn't."

Once my legs were securely bound, he returned to my arms, taping them again, making the binding much tighter. By the time he finished, nearly all the circulation to my hands had been cut off. While Shamus was doing this, Otto was doing the same thing to my legs. He also made the tape much tighter, cutting off the circulation to them as well. Almost immediately, my hands and feet went numb.

At this point, I was bound head to toe. Otto reached into my pockets and started taking out my belongings—my wallet, car keys and anything else of value he could find. Putting them in his pocket, Otto glared at me with an emotionless expression. Then, without altering his appearance in any way, he slid his finger across his throat, telling me exactly how they intended to murder me.

Seeing the frightened look on my face, Shamus added, "Otto has killed people before, Steve. He will do it again."

In my terror, I wet my pants. I couldn't help it.

Just so you know, being imprisoned not only confines your body, but also messes with your mind. It creates myriad negative, emotionally debilitating thoughts. Some of them you've probably never had before, but once they are there, they never go away. They become your constant, unwanted companion.

Seeing that I had pissed my pants infuriated Shamus. Coming so near to my face that I could smell his rancid alcoholic breath, he hissed. "You hear that, prick? You're not getting out of this alive."

Backing off about a foot to gain leverage, he slapped me across the face with an open hand that snapped my neck and turned my face. It stung like hell. I felt the blood rush to the left side of my face. Once Shamus started slapping me, he didn't stop. He struck me again and again, slapping me as hard as he could. Stopping to take a breath, he spit in my face. The smell of his spit was so nasty that I almost vomited.

Taking a long pull on his glass of *Jameson's* rejuvenated Shamus' strength, so he continued slapping and punching me, giving full vent to his rage. He was like a ravenous animal, ripping apart its hapless prey. When he finished beating me, which was only because he was too tired to continue, he started to curse me in every way imaginable. Shamus also cursed God, Christ and Christianity with the most foul-mouthed language imaginable. In his rage, exacerbating his level of drunken insanity, he yelled, "I'm not going to Heaven! I'm with the Devil now! That bitch, Mary!"

Seeing how out of control he had become was more frightening than the beating I had just endured. It wasn't just that Shamus was furious or even filled with rage. It was worse than that. I actually felt an evil presence in the room. Darkness began to encompass everything. I actually experienced a cold chill that was palpable even though the room, which lacked ventilation or air-conditioning, was stiflingly hot.

Reinvigorated by his rant or empowered by being possessed, Shamus returned to hitting me repeatedly. While doing so, he screamed, "You're a dead man! I am going to kill you."

I believed him.

I thought his rage had reached its zenith but I was mistaken. In fact, my situation became substantially worse. Instead of general threats to kill me, he became much more specific about how he was going to accomplish his task. "I'm going to cut you up starting with your fingers," he stated with wild, possessed eyes that danced with delight.

Taking the scissors he had used to bind me, he pulled my right forefinger away from the others, placing it between the blades of the scissors.

I braced myself, knowing I was about to experience intense pain, but then Shamus stopped. Having formed a better idea in his mind, he said, "You know what? I'll just cut your balls off instead."

"No!" I yelled, but my protestation only emboldened him.

A moment later, he knelt down to perform genital surgery on me. Since my legs were already spread apart and tied tightly, there was nothing I could do to stop him. Nevertheless, instinctively, I strained as hard as I could but I couldn't close my legs—not even by an inch. As he started to open and close the scissors between my legs, I shut my eyes and prayed for strength. Again, nothing happened.

While my eyes were closed, I grimaced. With a tortured expression on my face, I heard the sound of scissors clipping repeatedly, but the sound wasn't coming from between my legs. I could tell they were millimeters away from my eardrum. If I flinched or made even the smallest move, I knew he would cut off my ears. With my eyes remaining closed, feeling numb and dazed, I didn't move a muscle.

A few seconds later, Shamus threw the scissors on the floor. When he did, I opened my eyes and watched him leave the room. His leaving gave me no measure of comfort. For me, each moment was one of terror and anticipated horror. Within two minutes, Shamus returned from downstairs with his broken glass and a malevolent expression on his face. Evidently, he had settled on what he intended to do.

"I'm going to cut your eyes out. Then, I'm going to fuck your face up so badly no one will recognize you. Once I'm done, Otto is going to beat you to death while I watch."

Intent on blinding me, Shamus raised the broken glass and brought it down to my face. Lucky for me, at the last second, Otto blocked his advance. Instead of allowing Shamus to blind me, Otto dragged him out of the room by his arms with Shamus kicking and thrashing.

Looking at me, as he was being pulled away, Shamus screamed, "You're a dead man, Steve! Do you understand? I'm going to fucking kill you!"

A moment later, the door slammed shut and I was left alone to contemplate my death.

Chapter 17

Extortion

A fter Otto pushed Shamus out of the room, sparing my sight and perhaps my life by doing so, the younger man closed the door. When he did, I was alone with nothing but my terror-filled thoughts to keep me company. Although there were some good aspects to this, there were also some difficult ones. On the plus side, at least I wasn't being beaten and I still had my eyesight—thanks to Otto's intervention.

On the down side, it became nearly impossible to deal with my apprehensions. My abductors had gone too far with me. They needed to kill me and I knew it. Realizing this rattled me to the core of my being. What other choice did they have?

I know I've described the physical aspects of my torture quite well, but this was just part of what happened to me. The psychological torture that accompanied it was even worse. Otto had not only broken my ribs; he and Shamus had also broken my spirit. I don't think they understood the gravity of what they had done to me. Even I didn't comprehend the dynamics of it at the time.

The Steve Sarkela who entered Shamus' house of his own free will that evening has ceased to exist. Instead of being strong, resourceful and self-assured, which were character attributes ascribed to me by nearly everyone before that evening, I have become timid, apprehensive and inordinately cautious. In many ways, I have become a shell of the man I used to be.

Perhaps I can explain it best by using the example of what happens to a dog that has been beaten mercilessly. When this happens, the dog's spirit is broken and it cowers from then on. Even if a new owner treats it with love, care and compassion, the damage to the dog's spirit can't be undone. The dog may thrive and lead a good life, but there is a part of its nature that will forever remain fearful and apprehensive. It's why the dog tucks its tail between its legs when responding to its name.

Similarly, this is what Shamus and Otto did to me that night. While trying to rob me of money, they also stripped me of many basic character qualities. The loss of these non-tangibles cannot be quantified because these are things that can never be replaced or restored. Worse than robbing me of money, which can be replaced, Shamus and Otto deprived me of my ability to be the happy, carefree man I had always been. After my attack and subsequent torture, I was no longer able to enjoy life the way I once did.

Terrorist survivors understand the psychological nature of what happened to me. So do others who have been tortured. Sadly, this even happens to people who have been in abusive marriages. Abused individuals experience subtle changes that occur over time. Mine came in a rush and they were brutal and irreversible. One day, I was strong and self-confident. The next, I had become nervous and fearful.

As I sat there that evening, in my faux electric chair with nothing but my apprehensions to keep me company, the pain in my hands and feet became unbearable. With nearly all of the circulation having been cut off, they were cold, swollen and throbbed badly. Although I wanted to move them, my constraints wouldn't allow it. Nevertheless, I tried repeatedly. What else could I do?

My eyes burned too. I wanted desperately to rub them and wipe the sweat away—but I couldn't. To make matters worse,

I felt bloody sweat ooze onto my left eyebrow from one of the vicious blows to my head. Normally, experiencing this level of desperation would make me want to scream, but I didn't even have the energy or strength of will to do that. Besides, if I did, I suspected one or both of them would return to beat me some more. I certainly didn't want that.

The only thing in me that seemed to be moving freely was my heart and it was moving too fast. It was pounding so hard that I had to force myself to take measured breaths. Fearful of having a heart attack, I knew I needed to calm down. By then, my body had begun to shake uncontrollably and it became harder to calm down.

The air in the claustrophobic room, which had no ventilation, was stale and so hot that I was drenched with sweat. In an attempt to rest, I tried to lean my head against the wall but it was too far away from my chair to be comfortable.

Needless to say, I was as miserable as I could possibly be while waiting for my captors to determine my fate. During this time, I prayed to God more than I had prayed to Him in the past few years combined.

Feeling certain that Shamus and Otto were going to kill me, I didn't want them to get away with their heinous crime. Although dehydrated and close to passing out from heat exhaustion, I gathered as much saliva and blood in my mouth as I could. Then, using all of the energy I could muster, I spit on the wall. My goal was to make a mark that would leave something behind. This was all I could do, the last card I had to play. Unlike MacGyver, I didn't have a paperclip that I could use to save myself. My only hope was that the police would discover my bloody spit and provide conclusive DNA evidence that Shamus and Otto had been responsible for killing me.

Every hour, Otto checked on me just to make sure I was still alive. He opened the door and peered in while never saying a word. I asked him for some water but he never gave me any.

He never even responded to my request. Ignoring me, he just shut the door and left me sitting there, bound head to toe while wasting away from dehydration.

On one of his visits, I begged him to leave the door open just a little, because it was so hot. I was surprised he did and I was grateful. The next time he checked on me, he said nothing and closed the door after him, leaving me to continue suffocating in that dark, smelly room.

Quite a while later, I heard someone start a car. The vehicle moved from the front of the house, through the yard and all the way to the back. Because I recognized the noise of the engine, I knew it was my BMW. Putting two and two together, I knew they had made their decision about what to do with me. My time of waiting was close to being over and I wondered if my life was close to ending as well.

～⁓–––––◇–––––⁓～

From being constrained for so long without water, I lost consciousness for a while or maybe I just drifted off to sleep. In my sleep, the pain from my arms and legs became so unbearable I awoke in agony. It was awful. After what seemed like a long time, Otto and Shamus came back to the room. Otto was holding the big kitchen knife. Pulling back my head, he put it to my throat.

Coming very close to my face, Shamus asked, "Someone named Daniel keeps calling and texting you. Who is he?"

"My son," I told Shamus, barely able to speak.

"Where is he?" Shamus asked.

"He's at the hotel."

"What hotel?"

"The Hilton Garden Inn," I answered

"Which one?" He demanded.

"The one by the airport," I replied truthfully, knowing that Daniel would never open the door for Otto, if that happened to be what Shamus had in mind. Although I certainly wasn't safe, my son was—thank God.

Interrupting my thought, Shamus looked at me menacingly. After a long moment, he said, "Okay, this is how it's going to work. We're going to untie you and you're going to call him. When you do, you're going to say exactly what we tell you to say. Do you understand?"

"Yes," I replied feebly, but all I could think about was how grateful I would be to finally be able to move my hands and feet.

"You can't say anything else," he added. Being very specific, Shamus warned, "If you give him any hint about what has happened, if you tell him to call for help or if you even say the word 'police,' Otto will slit your throat. Do you understand, Steve?"

"Yes," I replied.

"Otto's knife is never going to leave your neck. Got it?"

"Got it," I affirmed weakly.

A moment later, Shamus began to untie me. Being bound as thoroughly as I was, it took him quite a while. While Shamus was busy doing this, Otto continued to hold the knife to my throat, which was very disconcerting. With Shamus pulling and tugging at the tape and cotton strands as hard as he was, I was concerned Otto might inadvertently cut my throat. It didn't happen.

Once I was free, they stood me up. Even standing, after having been constrained for so long, was a difficult task. As the blood returned to my hands and feet, which took quite a few seconds, I became less wobbly. At last, I was able to take a step ... then another, eventually gaining my balance and equilibrium. I was now able to walk but each step was painful. Without providing me with even a drop of water, they brought me downstairs to Shamus office. Once there, they sat me in his chair, which was behind a large desk. The two of them stood behind me.

Because my throat was so dry, my voice was barely audible. It was no more than a whisper. Realizing that I wouldn't sound normal talking this way, they finally gave me a bottle of water, which had been sitting nearby.

You cannot imagine how wonderful that water tasted. Putting the bottle to my mouth, I drank every drop of it despite having an unsteady hand.

Shamus then handed me my phone, which I could see had been reassembled. Taking it, I saw that Daniel had called me five times and texted me more often than that. Hitting the redial button, Daniel picked up immediately.

"Dad?" He said.

It was wonderful to hear his voice, especially since there was a strong possibility I would never hear it again.

"Daniel," I answered, trying to sound as normal as possible, but it was difficult not to burst into tears. Knowing it might cost me my life, I fought back my tears valiantly.

"Are you okay?" Daniel asked. From his tone and intimation, I could tell he was very concerned about me. I knew this just by the way he called my name. Before I could respond, he added, "You don't sound good. What's going on? Can you drive? When are you coming back?" He asked all of these questions in rapid fire without giving me an opportunity to answer one of them before asking me the next.

"I'm fine, Daniel," I replied, trying to calm him down. "We're just finishing up here. Go to sleep."

"Okay," he replied, easily satisfied.

A moment later, he asked, "Hey, can you bring me some food when you come back to the hotel? I'm starving."

"Sure," I answered. "Now go to sleep and I'll take care of everything."

"Okay, Dad. Bye." With that, he hung up.

Mission accomplished. I had done what I had been required to do but it took everything in me not to blurt out what Shamus and Otto were doing. More than anything, I didn't want to bring my son into this murderous situation. Since Shamus was content to leave Daniel out of it, so was I.

After the call, Otto stood guard over me with the knife. Talking about stabbing me through the skull with it and mimicking his best martial arts technique, he wanted to make sure that I remained intimidated. While Otto brandished the knife, Shamus scurried around the room collecting papers. Returning to the desk, he slapped them down in front of me, then handed me a pen.

"Sign them or else," he hissed.

Picking them up, I glanced at them. They were deed transfer documents for the seven condominiums.

"Don't read them!" Shamus barked. "Just sign them!" With that, he pointed to the signature line.

Picking up the pen, I complied, signing the first one.

Taking the document I had just signed, Otto looked at my signature.

"Sign your full name," Otto demanded. That I followed his instructions seemed very important to him.

For some reason unknown by me, Shamus and Otto argued about the way I signed my name to each document they placed in front of me. Their quarrelling took quite a while. After so many years of signing closing documents and other business-related records, my signature had become little more than scribble—just like a doctor's signature.

Shamus looked over the documents I had signed by comparing my signature to the one on my driver's license. Smiling, with a self-satisfied smirk, he said, "The signatures look good."

Once I was finished signing, Otto, being the witness, read and signed the transfer documents. Upon completing the task, Shamus said he had some kind of insurance that would keep me from getting him in trouble for what he had just done. This surprised me, since I had never heard of any insurance policy that covered kidnapping—not for the kidnapper—but I kept this thought to myself for obvious reasons.

"Excellent," Shamus said with a twisted smile, having successfully stolen more than one million dollars in property from me. "I want the money for the property that is about to close too." He then added, "Just so that you don't cause any trouble for us, I'm going to put you in jail for breaking into my home."

I wasn't sure what he was talking about. He handed Otto my phone and wallet then left the room. Otto remained with me, guarding me with the knife.

Just a minute or two later, I heard the front doorbell ring. It lifted my spirits. I suspected that someone must have called the police but what happened next became the most surprising event of the evening.

Chapter 18

Wicked Twist of Fate

A few seconds after the front door bell rang, I could hear Shamus shuffling to the door. The second ring was followed by persistent knocking. It was clear the person on the front porch had authority of some kind. Shamus then answered the door and I could hear two muffled voices even though I was too far away to understand what they were saying. The man at the door was very insistent and did not intend to be put off.

Even though I considered screaming, I didn't. Frankly, as weak as I was, I wasn't sure I would be able to yell loud enough to be heard. Suspecting I might have something like this in mind, Otto pressed the blade of the knife against my neck quite a bit harder. Although his move had been forceful, it wasn't powerful enough to break the skin.

A moment later, a police officer entered the room followed closely behind by Shamus. My immediate thought was to thank God, thinking my nightmare was finally over. I had survived the ordeal. I hoped the officer would come to my aid, immediately call for backup and arrest my two abductors—but that's not what happened.

That's not even close to what happened.

Just before the policeman entered the room, Otto removed the knife from my throat so it looked like I was just sitting there waiting for the authorities to arrive. Once the policeman saw me, he approached cautiously. I noticed his right hand was hovering over his gun—like he was a gunslinger in the Old West, ready to draw on me at the slightest provocation. Witnessing this was very surprising and equally disturbing. It was obvious the cop considered me to be a threat, which I certainly wasn't. Although I couldn't imagine what in the world was going on, my bewilderment didn't last long.

Speaking to me very sternly, the officer commanded; "Keep your hands to your sides." Once I obeyed, he added, "Now go stand in the corner."

Although his order confused me, it was crystal clear. I complied with his command immediately—not deviating from it in any way. Getting up, despite being very stiff, which was exacerbated by the enormous pain I had been forced to endure, I walked to the edge of the room and faced the corner precisely as I had been instructed. It was like I was seven years old and being punished by my mother for some childish prank. The entire situation seemed bizarre and surreal.

A moment later, the officer walked up behind me. Coming so close to my right ear that I could smell the Skoal on his breath, he asked, "Are you carrying a weapon?"

Confused by his question, I answered, "What?" A brief moment later, I added, "No, I'm not."

Bewildered, I couldn't imagine why he would ask me such a thing, but it became apparent immediately. While I was standing there, he gave me a pat down, being careful to not touch the part of my trousers that were still damp from urine. Once he finished, being satisfied I didn't have a weapon, he grabbed my shoulders firmly, turned me around quickly and looked at me with hostility.

Once I was facing him, the officer asked, "Why are you robbing this house?" Not giving me the opportunity to answer, he asked a second question. "Have you stolen from other houses in this neighborhood before tonight?"

I opened my mouth to speak but was unable to articulate anything discernable. Nothing would come out. I was emotionally distressed but the officer misinterpreted my reticence to speak as defiance. Instead of viewing me as an injured victim, he perceived my silence as an act of belligerence and he didn't like it at all. In fact, he became antagonistic towards me quickly. Grabbing me roughly, he pushed me out of Shamus' office into the foyer, where a second officer was standing.

"Give me your driver's license," the second officer demanded. If anything, he was more confrontational than the first.

Knowing better than to refuse his clear directive in any way, I opened my wallet and began rummaging through it for my driver's license. Shaking from head to toe, I fumbled around still wondering if I was having a bad dream, but knowing I wasn't. I dug through every one of my credit cards, pictures and receipts looking for my license.

Shamus and Otto, having gone through my wallet earlier, had simply crammed everything back into it without any order. This made locating my license cumbersome, which continued to irritate the two policemen.

It required several minutes for me to find it. By that time, two more police cars arrived. This meant four or five police officers were now standing around me in the entryway. All of them seemed to have one thing in common—a loathsome disdain for me. This was quite intimidating, of course, particularly since it was completely unwarranted.

One officer asked, "Are you on drugs?" He wasn't the only one who wanted to know this. I was asked several times but I was never allowed to answer. Finally, I stopped trying to speak and simply shook my head. Even this was difficult, because my head hurt so much from the assault.

Looking at me contemptuously, the first officer asked, "What are you doing here?" Again, not allowing me to answer, he asked a second and third question in rapid fire. "What did you take from the house?" Following this by, "Is anyone with you?"

Every time I was addressed by one of the officers, they spoke to me condescendingly. You can't imagine how intimidating that was. From their perspective, since they believed they were addressing a thief, they didn't need to be respectful. Nor did they need to be kind either.

While I was undergoing this interrogation, Shamus and Otto stood close by—hovering less than ten feet away. They were doing their best to pay attention to what I was being asked and how I answered the questions. Still fearful of what Shamus and Otto might say or do to me, I asked the first officer, "Can we talk outside?" When I said this, it may have been the first complete sentence I had been allowed to speak without being interrupted.

Surprised, the first officer looked at his partner who must have been senior to him on the force. The second officer replied, "Sure, follow me."

I followed the policeman, as he walked purposefully outside, doing my best not to make eye contact with either Otto or Shamus. Despite doing this, I could still feel their malice. It was like a force field boring a hole in the back of my head.

The officer walked to the driveway, stopped, turned around and looked at me intensely. Because he had treated me roughly inside, I had no alternative but to be honest with him.

Whispering, I said to him, "I can't talk here."

"Why not?" the officer asked. Immediately afterwards, he asked, "Are you on drugs?"

As he was saying this, I turned my head slightly and caught a glimpse of Shamus through the window. He was laughing and I saw him pat one of the officers on the back. Seeing this not only made me feel sick, it also made me nervous. It looked like Shamus and the cop were personal friends, making me wonder if the police had been compromised. Seeing this made me fearful and forced me to be cautious.

After witnessing how chummy Shamus was with the policeman, I decided that I couldn't trust the Mount Pleasant Police Department. So, I decided not to tell them what had actually happened. Choosing to be circumspect rather than foolhardy, I decided to call my lawyer first. I needed to get his advice before relating my story. Right on the spot, I decided it was the only prudent thing to do.

Addressing the officer, I said, "Never mind."

By refusing to speak, this worsened my situation substantially. The cop looked at me like I was crazy, or worse, and he became convinced I was on drugs. Thinking this must be the reason for my bizarre behavior, when the other officers came outside, they gave me three separate field sobriety tests.

Being quite rough with me, they pushed me around saying, "Stand here." A moment later they would yell, "No, stand over there!" hooping, hollering and laughing as they did. It was awful. They tried their best to agitate me but I knew better than to allow them to get the better of me. Having already been beaten mercilessly for hours, I refused to do anything or say anything that might justify one of them using his nightstick on me. Despite being compliant to each of their orders, they continued to taunt and harass me. Honestly, they acted more like a gang of bullies than real policemen. They goaded me repeatedly, making sport of everything I did.

While this was happening, several other police cars arrived. In all, at one time or another, there must have been at least ten police officers at the house. Eventually, the police lieutenant arrived and headed directly to me. He grabbed me roughly and started pushing me around. He then pointed his finger in my face and screamed at me.

With a look of pure hatred, he said, "If this was my home, I would have shot you dead! There would be a white line around your body. Do you know what that means?"

Although I knew better than to open my mouth in response, I definitely understood what that meant. His goal was to agitate me, hoping to escalate the situation. Knowing this would put me at risk to further bodily harm, I wisely kept my wits about me. Seeing that I could not be provoked to resist him, he finally stopped, much to my relief.

A few minutes later, after all the cops huddled together, one of the officers wrote me a "No Trespassing Notice." Eventually, after handing it to me, he said I was free to leave.

I was shocked and surprised when he said that I could leave. I was certain I would be arrested, but I wasn't. Despite how inappropriately I had been treated and how badly I had been misunderstood, I can't tell you how relieved I was to hear those words from the cop. I could leave. I was free to go. It was almost too good to be true. Earlier, I had been certain I would not survive the night, but I had. Shortly after the police arrived, I felt sure I would be arrested, but that didn't happen either. Although I was in pain from head to toe, I was grateful to be alive and I thanked God for His protection.

With my "No Trespassing Notice" in one hand and my car keys in the other, I headed for my BMW but it wasn't where I had parked it. Then I remembered Shamus had moved it earlier.

"Where is my car parked?" I asked one of the cops, trying to give him a subtle hint about what had happened. When he looked at me, I added, "It was parked in the front when I came."

Apparently, my hint was too subtle for this moron. It went straight over his head, which shouldn't have surprised me given how they had consistently misjudged the situation. There was no response as several policemen continued to talk to Shamus. Against my better judgment, I decided to try again—this time a little louder. "Who moved my car?" I demanded.

Although it was clear they heard me this time, they completely ignored me. To them, I was a criminal and not worth the effort to respond.

Giving up, I started to look for my car around the house. I finally found it parked in the backyard against a hedge. To get in, I had to climb over the console from the passenger side. I didn't want to ruin the leather upholstery with stains from my urine or my blood.

Starting the car, I drove off slowly, fearful that I might be stopped if it looked like I was trying to "get away." Because I had been tied up for so long, my right foot shook while I drove. I was in considerable pain, which made everything I did more difficult.

Despite all that had happened, I was alive and I was free. Having been convinced I would never see my son again, I couldn't wait to see Daniel. I headed back to the Hilton Garden Inn, grimacing in pain from even the slightest movement I had to make while driving.

Chapter 19

Go Straight to the FBI

lthough the drive back to the hotel required twenty minutes, it took me nearly thirty. It wasn't because there were any traffic delays—not at that time of night. It's because I circled around numerous time just to make sure I wasn't being followed. I didn't think I had been, but I certainly wasn't an expert on surveillance techniques.

Seeing how supportive the police had been to Shamus and Otto was very disconcerting. It made me wonder if I could trust anybody in Charleston. I would never have suspected anything like this could have happened—never in a million years—but it had.

I had been ruthlessly attacked, tortured and nearly murdered, but the Mount Pleasant Police Department didn't do a thing to come to my defense. They didn't protect me. Instead, although keenly aware of how badly I had been beaten, which was obvious by the cuts and bruises all over my body, they chose to side with my attackers. They even joined in on my intimidation and humiliation rather than performing their sworn duty.

Arriving at the Hilton Garden Inn, I parked the BMW and looked around to make certain I wasn't going to be attacked again. Numb and dazed, I took the elevator to our floor and fumbled through my pockets for the room key. I took another look around just to be safe. Then I opened the door and locked it quickly behind me, fastening the deadbolt. After checking to make sure no one else was in the room, I looked over at Daniel who was sound asleep.

Thanking the Lord for protecting him, I let out a sigh of relief. Although my body was weak and shaking from dehydration and exhaustion, I went to the bathroom and drank two glasses of water. Nothing ever tasted so good as that tap water. It also made me feel better, rejuvenating me immediately.

Next, I started to clean my body slowly and methodically, wiping away blood, sweat and spit. All of my clothing was soiled and bloody. My golf shirt was torn and covered with dried blood. Once I took off my damp pants, I knew I would never put them back on again. Besides, they were torn in several places.

If I had been thinking clearly, which I wasn't, I would have used my iPhone to take numerous selfies, showing the extent of my wounds, but I didn't. My desire to take a shower and wash myself off was too great.

Believe it or not, it was even painful to run warm water over my head, but feeling clean was at that moment, the best feeling in the world. After my shower, I examined myself in the mirror and took a thorough inventory of my wounds. At the same time, I also tried to remember and reconstruct the events that caused them.

First, I noticed a large bump on my head that occurred when I hit a solid wooden bench after being kicked by Otto. Next, on the left side of my head, I found another bump. This was caused by a karate punch to my temple. Because it caused a stinging sensation whenever I moved my jaw, this was one of my most painful injuries. As a result, I had trouble eating for weeks. It hurt to chew. My left eye was almost shut and continued to swell while the skin above it remained split and oozing blood. Looking at it closely reminded me of the way Rocky looked after going fifteen rounds with Apollo Creed. I definitely knew how the Italian Stallion felt. My back was stiff and aching in several places. Not to mention, my stomach and ribs felt even worse. My stomach was bruised but this didn't concern me nearly as much as the pain in my ribs. Since I couldn't breathe deeply, I suspected several of them were cracked.

I had so many wounds and bruises that I lost count. Honestly, my entire body felt like one large sore. Despite my discomfort, I was exhausted. Although it was becoming increasingly difficult to move, even after having showered, I knew I needed to get some rest. Taking two extra strength painkillers, I collapsed on the bed but couldn't fall asleep. I kept thinking about everything that had happened, replaying the events over and over in my mind.

I tossed and turned. Although I was safe, I didn't feel safe. Being in the presence of such evil and unable to flee, the core of my being had been rattled. Being attacked like that did more than make me fear for my life. It destroyed a part of my soul more effectively than Otto's blows had broken my physical body. My emotions were shattered.

Despite being in a locked room, with a chair propped up against a bolted door in a hotel, I worried about my safety and Daniel's too. My apprehension wasn't grounded in reality, of course, but it felt real nonetheless. Shamus and Otto's intimidation penetrated my soul, unnerving me and the wounds this caused have required much longer to heal than my bodily injuries. In many ways, I still haven't healed and fear I never will.

When I was young, I was noted for being carefree. I am no longer that person. That part of me, my happy-go-lucky spirit, has vanished. Instead, my nature has become extremely cautious— not about everything—but certainly about being physically safe. My abduction and torture became life transforming. Eventually, I came to realize that I would never be the same person I had once been. It simply wasn't possible.

That night, however, I didn't understand any of this. All I knew was that I remained fearful that Shamus and Otto would break through the door and kill Daniel and me. Finally drifting off, I awakened soon thereafter. This was a pattern that was replicated for the rest of the night. I would fall asleep but awaken soon afterwards, filled with fear and trepidation. It was awful. I doubt I had two hours of sleep but as exhausted as I was, I couldn't have been more grateful for the little sleep I got that night.

I was wide-awake at 6 a.m. the following morning despite my exhaustion. Getting out of bed, I called my brother, Rodney, knowing he would be up and about. Explaining what happened in detail, he made me promise to go to the police and file a report. While I was talking to him, I looked in the bathroom mirror and was shocked by how badly I looked. My right eye was nearly swollen shut and blood still oozed from several places, including my head and eyebrow.

Awakening Daniel, I explained to him what happened in abbreviated terms.

We were both famished, having not eaten for almost 18 hours. We had breakfast in the room then headed out to file a police report.

While we were en route to the police station, Daniel turned to me and asked, "Dad, what if the police we talk to are in on this with Shamus and Otto?"

His question stopped me dead in my tracks. A pang of fear pierced my stomach, nearly making my heart miss a beat. Daniel was right. I couldn't afford to make another mistake. Uncertain about what to do, I called Duffy Tipton—Pelican Gulf's lawyer. Although Duffy didn't practice criminal law, he was the only lawyer I knew. Being the case, his advice would have to suffice. I had no other choice.

Answering my call almost immediately, I informed Duffy about the entire episode and left nothing out. When I finished,

I looked over at Daniel, whose eyes and mouth were wide open. Having heard a detailed version of my attack, he realized my assault was far more serious than he had originally thought it was. In an instant, I could see a transformation in my son.

As he listened to the details, his countenance changed. This was no longer a game for him. Instead, sitting there, he prepared himself for the task ahead. He was going to be my sidekick as we sought justice together.

On the other end of the call, having no idea what had silently passed between my son and me, Duffy thought about the seriousness of what I had disclosed for a minute. Having made a decision about how to advise me, he took the lead in our conversation.

Being direct and forceful, Duffy exhorted. "Steve, do not go in the police station. They cannot help you and probably won't even try. Go straight to the FBI."

"The FBI?" I replied, clearly surprised by his counsel.

"Yes, that's precisely what you need to do. Call the FBI immediately."

Having pulled into a parking lot to talk, I thanked Duffy for his help and hung up. Using my iPhone to search for the local office of the Federal Bureau of Investigation, I found the location and phone number quickly.

Calling immediately, after just one ring, a pleasant sounding receptionist answered. "May I help you?" she asked.

"Yes, you can," I responded. "Someone is trying to kill me."

"Sir, this is the FBI—not your local police," she responded politely. She added, "But, I can give you that number, if you ..." she continued, fully intent on directing my call to the local police department—the one I was sure was in collusion with Shamus.

I interrupted her. "I can't go there! They won't help me."

"Why not?" she asked.

Answering her, I stated, "Because they are helping the criminals, that's why." Certain she was now engaged and interested, I started to tell her what happened.

Halfway through my story, she stopped me. "I'm going to get an agent on the line," she said. A moment later, she put me on hold.

After listening to soothing background music for a while—a long while—a man finally picked up the phone. "This is Special Agent Sterling Wright. May I help you?"

"I sure hope so, Agent Wright," I replied.

I then told him about how two men had tried to extort me. I explained that they had beaten me and threatened to kill me if they didn't get the deeds to my condos. I also told him they demanded that I give them the money I was about to receive from the sale of a condo that was about to close.

After listening to me for a while, he instructed me to come to his office in an hour. When he said this, I felt a sense of hope knowing the FBI was on the case. Something good was about to happen. I was sure of it and I was glad to be fighting back ... finally.

Chapter 20

Believe Me, Agent Wright

P romptly, at 10 a.m., I walked into the building that housed the FBI. As I looked at the marquis, I noticed that this was also the building where the U.S. Marshalls were located, along with numerous other governmental agencies. Finding the correct floor, Daniel and I got into the elevator and went up.

Ringing the buzzer that was outside the FBI's office, there was a small beep and the door unlocked. After we entered, the door closed behind us with a click, locking us in. Normally, this might have been intimidating, but not this time. Hearing that sound made me feel safe and secure for the first time since being introduced to Otto's fist.

Walking in, we had to pass through a metal detector. Once we did, we gained entry to the lobby. The room had a receptionist who sat behind a very thick glass partition, sealing her away from us completely.

Smiling, she asked, "What was your name again?"

"Steve Sarkela," I said. "I'm the guy you spoke with earlier— the guy who called for an appointment with Agent Sterling Wright."

"I remember," she said with a smile, appraising me. I must have looked like hell, being beaten up as badly as I was, but she didn't mention it. Instead, she smiled. "Have a seat. Agent Wright will be with you shortly."

"Thank you," I said, as both Daniel and I took a seat in the waiting room. A while later, Daniel and I were led into an interrogation room. I was sure this was what it was because there were steel bars on the walls designed to attach handcuffs. In the center of the room, there was a round metal table with four chairs. The walls were white and completely bare. It was reminiscent of a lab, with the white walls and all the metal. It looked very antiseptic. After waiting for nearly an hour, a man entered the room.

"Hello, I'm Agent Sterling Wright," he said, introducing himself with a smile. Turning to Daniel, he said, "Would you mind waiting in the lobby while your dad and I talk?"

"No, sir," Daniel responded. Picking up his Game Boy, he headed to the lobby. After he left, Agent Wright sat across from me on opposite sides of the table.

After a brief silence, he asked, "So why are you here?"

Not needing to be coaxed, I began to tell my story. I made sure to be very descriptive about the beating I received at the hands of Otto and Shamus. While I was explaining what had happened, he stopped me.

"Wait, where did this happen?" Wright asked.

"In Mount Pleasant—no more than two or three miles from here."

Surprised by my response, Wright pulled out a pad and began taking notes. Seeing how serious he was taking this, I continued with my story but he interrupted me again.

"Are you alright?" he asked. "You look like you've had a hard night." Evaluating me, he added, "We can forget about this if you want to leave. You are free to go."

Hearing him say this surprised me. Responding, I said, "But I don't want to leave. This is the first place I've felt safe since the attack."

Although he wasn't angry, his next response was very direct and a little confrontational. "Mr. Sarkela, you are in a federal building, speaking with an agent of the FBI." Being very clear and professional, he counseled me, "It is a federal crime to lie to the FBI. You can leave right now, but if this case goes any further, you might not be able to leave." Looking at me intensely, he added, "I want to be perfectly clear with you about this—just so you understand."

"I understand, Agent Wright," I affirmed, being just as clear and direct as he was. "I'm not leaving. I'm serious about this. Everything happened—just the way I've described it to you."

Once I said this, he simply nodded his head, took his legal pad and pen and began writing. Starting from the beginning, which he directed me to do, I went over everything again, explaining each event numerous times. Meticulously pouring over the details of my story, I stayed in that interrogation room with him nearly all day.

At one point, I asked, "Should I just pay Shamus what he wants so that I can stay safe?"

"No," Agent Wright answered emphatically. "That would only make things worse. He will just come back for more and when all the money is gone, he will be more likely to kill you."

Wright's response definitely unnerved me.

Returning to an earlier point, he asked, "Tell me again about the police that came. Were they city police?"

"I'm not positive," I replied, "but the sides of their cars said Mount Pleasant."

Wright was surprised the Mount Pleasant Police were involved and disappointed in how unprofessionally they handled the situation. He asked, "Why didn't they arrest you?"

"I have no idea. That surprised me too," I admitted. Then, I remembered that I had the ticket. Pulling it out of my pocket, I handed the crumpled piece of paper to him. "They just gave me this and told me I could leave."

Taking the ticket, Wright looked it over. "What is this?" he asked, clearly surprised by what I had been given. It says, "'You are not to come within 1000 feet of this property for a period of one year or you will be arrested.'"

Reading it a second time, with flared nostrils, I could see that Agent Wright had become angry.

Looking at me, clearly vexed, he said, "They don't have the authority to write a notice like this or to write any restraining order."

When he saw my ticket, it was the turning point in the interview. Until then, he hadn't been invested—not really—but now he was. At that precise moment, Agent Wright believed my story and I knew I finally had an advocate. With him leading the way, the FBI took charge of the case.

Looking at me, he said, "I'm going to have a detective look into the Mount Pleasant Police." Obviously, I was interested in what Wright's agent discovered, but we never talked about the Mount Pleasant Police Department again. I brought it up numerous times, but they brushed me off just as often, always changing the subject. Obviously, they didn't want to disparage another law enforcement agency.

Agent Wright definitely wanted to know everything I knew about Shamus and Otto, so I withheld nothing. I told the agent everything I knew. While I was providing details, another man entered the room. Agent Wright introduced him as Special Agent Nathan Hawthorne.

They began questioning me about Otto. "Did you see what he looked like?" Wright asked.

I explained what I knew, which wasn't much. They asked if he had any distinguishing marks, tattoos or anything unusual about his face?

Responding, I confessed, "I tried not to look at him too much." I added, "I kept my eyes on the floor most of the time, hoping he wouldn't cut my throat."

When I said this, both agents' eyes lit up at once. Agent Hawthorne said, "If you were looking at the floor, you must have seen his shoes."

"Yeah, I did," I admitted. "They were different looking and he had tape wrapped around his foot."

"What about his pants?" Nathan asked.

"They were gym pants—exercise pants." I said.

"Okay, wait here," Agent Wright said, leaving the room.

Ten to fifteen minutes later, Wright came back with Otto's photo and complete identification, which surprised me. Smiling, in an effort to add a little humor to our intense proceedings, he said, "Don't feel bad about losing the fight, Steve. This guy's full name is Otto Z. Roddick and he's a black belt karate champion in Europe."

Hearing this, my mouth opened wide—at least as wide as I could without feeling too much pain. Looking at the papers Wright had thrown on the table in front of me, I thought about the fight and how vigorously I had defended myself. From what I had just learned, I felt better about myself knowing Otto was a professional fighter and three-time European Karate Champion.

<hr />

While I was in the interrogation room with Agents Wright and Hawthorne, Shamus O'Dunnigan called my cell phone and left a voicemail. He said that the closing did not go through and he was angry that he had not received "his money" from the sale.

Although I had intended to go to the closing myself, which was one of the reasons I had for making the trip, Shamus, who now had signed documents saying he was the seller, went instead. When he went to the closing, with papers in hand, he demanded that the funds be given to him. Since this isn't what the attorney or buyer expected, they became nervous and cancelled the closing, infuriating Shamus.

The FBI agents listened to the voicemail. When they did, they asked me to return Shamus' call. They wanted to record it and even coached me about what to say.

As you can imagine, I was very nervous returning Shamus' call, but after Agent Hawthorne attached the recording device to my cell phone, I sucked it up and placed the call.

"Shamus," I said, after he picked up.

"Yes, who is this?" he asked.

"It's me, Steve. I was ..." I started to say, but he interrupted me, practically shouting. This scared me, despite being safe inside FBI headquarters.

"Listen here!" Shamus growled, "You need to call that attorney and authorize her to give me the money from the closing."

"Okay I'll call her," I told him, trying to calm him down, but he had already gone over the edge.

Screaming at me, he threatened, "You'd better, Steve, if you know what's good for you. It's going to be worse than you can imagine if you don't. I'll do it! You hear me?"

"Yes," I replied weakly, shaken to the core. "I will call her and tell her to give you the money."

"Alright. Don't fuck this up or I'll finish the job," he added— just to make sure I was thoroughly intimidated. Knowing I was, he hung up without saying another word.

Panting, I was unnerved from having to deal with Shamus. Hearing his voice forced me to relive my torture from the previous night in my mind, but his call, which the FBI had recorded, was valuable. If there had been any doubt about the truthfulness of my story, hearing Shamus' threat to kill me dispelled them.

Shamus wasn't the only one who had been unsuccessful in trying to reach me. Having been in the interrogation room most of the day, telling and retelling my story, adding bits of clarifying information here and there, I had missed numerous calls. One was from the real estate agent for the buyer who called me repeatedly, wondering what in the world was happening. She also wondered if I was okay, which was nice of her.

Agent Hawthorne instructed me to ignore the realtor's call and said he would deal with her. After that, Agent Wright handed me a recording device, showing me how to use it—just in case Shamus called again. I had never seen anything like it before. It definitely didn't look like something that was a recorder.

After spending nearly the entire day at the FBI office, I didn't feel like going back to the hotel. Instead, Daniel and I went to my daughter's house. When we arrived, having talked to her uncle about what had happened to me, Olivia rushed out of the house to welcome me. She squeezed me so hard that it hurt my ribs.

"Dad, are you okay?" Olivia asked. "What's going on?"

Filling her in, I told her where Daniel and I had been for most of the day.

"Is the FBI going to arrest Shamus?" Olivia asked.

"They're working on it," I said. A moment later, I added, "I'm very tired."

Taking me by the hand to lead me into the house, with Daniel following close behind, Olivia continued bombarding me with questions. Being at my physical and emotional limit, having done nothing but answer questions for hours, I really didn't want to go through everything again. Although she knew this, Olivia pressed me for details. She couldn't help herself.

Finally, becoming insistent, she pleaded with me. "Dad, please talk to me."

With no alternative, I relented. Starting from the beginning, I went over everything, as Olivia's look of apprehension slowly transformed from concern to one of shock. It was clearly traumatizing for her to hear the story of her father being assaulted. When Milton, Olivia's husband, came home, I started over. Both listened intently. When I finished, we decided that Daniel and I would spend the night there and not return to the hotel.

After deciding to stay, I went into the bathroom and took my shirt off while Olivia got her camera. Just about every inch of my upper body was bruised and purple. My eye had swollen completely shut and was oozing slightly. The skin around my ribs looked more purple than white. I was a mess—no doubt about it—but the photographic evidence of my beating proved to be essential.

Saying goodnight, while getting ready for bed, I pulled out my gun. It was a loaded .40 caliber Glock and it never left my hand—not once.

Chapter 21

FBI Sting

O n Saturday morning, I woke up at around 7:00 a.m. still groggy because I didn't sleep soundly. I went downstairs and made myself a cup of coffee, which I needed desperately to wake up. A couple of hours later, with everybody up, Shamus called. Seeing who it was rattled me. It also made it difficult for me to remember what the FBI had instructed me to do. While my cell phone rang, I fumbled around before finally connecting my recording device.

I spoke into the recorder just as instructed. "This is Saturday, June 5, 2010, 9:00 a.m."

"Hello," I answered quickly, hopeful the call hadn't already transferred to voicemail.

"This is Shamus," my nemesis stated abruptly. Before I could speak, he yelled, "If you don't have the money for me on Monday, things are going to get a lot worse. What happened at the house is nothing compared to what will occur next time. I know all about your kids—all of them. Oh, and don't forget about your grandkids. I have people—bad people. They will find you and hurt all of you."

Having threatened my entire family, I found it hard to breathe, but Shamus wasn't done.

Although he had stopped for a long moment to allow what he said to sink in, he continued. "You know what will happen next, don't you? This all comes to an end if I don't get that money. I will hunt you down and kill you."

Without allowing me to respond in any way, Shamus hung up. My legs went slack and I felt weak. Truthfully, I thought I might wet my pants again. And thank God I didn't. Obviously, I was scared, but not just for me. Now I was terrified for my family too. Despite being intimidated, just like most people would be, I felt the need to respond. I had the urge to kill him. Thinking about how I could do it, I wondered if I could get away with it. I questioned if this was the only way I would find peace. Being so angry made my stomach upset, but I didn't have time to get sick. Instead, I needed to be strong and proactive—not just for myself but also for my family. Although they didn't know it, their lives depended on me to face this terrible evil and not shrink away from it.

Seizing the moment, I called Agent Hawthorne immediately. I told him about the phone call. He tried to calm me down but that was difficult. After listening to Shamus threaten my life, along with the lives of my family, being calm was next to impossible. Before disconnecting, Hawthorne told me I needed to return to his office in the federal building first thing on Monday morning.

Later on Saturday, Cynthia Bruner, another FBI agent called. We talked for a long time and she set up a meeting for me a few days later with an ex-CIA agent—a man who counseled victims of violent crimes.

I was blessed with a large family. All of my siblings and nearly all of my stepbrothers and stepsisters called to make sure I was okay. They also wanted to hear the story of what had happened directly from me. Needless to say, these conversations kept me busy, but I was also able to get some much-needed rest. The only one from my family who didn't call was my mother. She and Ahab were conspicuously silent. I didn't hear a peep from them.Nevertheless, the next afternoon, after having attended church, I decided to visit my mother and stepfather. Arriving at their residence, they greeted me in their customary manner. Although their demeanor was the same, it was obvious they were very nervous. Not expecting them to be, I was surprised.

Like everybody else, they wanted to hear what happened directly from me. While explaining my attack, my stepfather became quite nervous, perhaps even a little agitated, but not my mother. Although I was her son and had experienced a life-threatening attack at the hands of someone she knew quite well, Jezzy just sat there and listened—emotionless and almost indifferent to my plight. No warmth came from her—no tender caring for a son who had been attacked—just cold detachment.

I'm not sure what I expected, but I certainly didn't expect disinterest. Ahab didn't seem nearly as cold, at least at the beginning. When I gave him the details of my attack, he became very uneasy. Eventually, he left the room—never to return. While I continued to tell the story to my mom, I could see Ahab through the window pacing back and forth outside, deep in thought. While I was with them, neither showed me any compassion. This confused me. I desperately needed the support and encouragement of my family—especially my mother.

Because they had been doing business with Shamus O'Dunnigan for many years, I asked them to help me convict him of his many crimes against me. Handing Jezzy the business card of Agent Hawthorne, I asked her to call him. Hawthorne had given me the card for this specific purpose, to see if either of them would be willing to help the FBI on their own. When I handed her Agent Hawthorne's card, this was the only time I witnessed any emotion on my mother's face, but I couldn't tell whether her expression was one of fear or one of surprise. Seeing the blood drain from her face, I suspected it was fear.

With nothing further to say, I left.

The following day was the only other time my mother talked to me about the crime. Calling me early in the day, being very firm and direct, she said that I should not press charges against

Shamus. She added that it would be best for me to simply forget the whole thing. She cautioned me to not say another word about what happened—not to anyone.

I was flabbergasted, thinking she had lost her mind. I couldn't believe what she was advising me to do, but she was dead serious.

During the conversation, she said, "I am your mother, Steve. I know what is best for you. Forget about this and act like it never happened."

Being as emotionally traumatized as I was—practically a basket case, her admonition didn't sink in at the time, but I've thought about it hundreds of times since. Her advice was not just bizarre, it was also disturbing. Others in my family felt exactly the same way Jezzy did. Much later, several of my sisters asked me to drop the case against Shamus, which I wasn't about to do. I couldn't even if I had tried. None of them had any idea about what a federal crime entails. There was no way I could stop the process—nor did I want to. That was the last thing I wanted.

On Monday morning, as directed by Agent Hawthorne, I went to the FBI office in downtown Charleston, leaving Daniel at his sister's house. Pushing the button, just like I had done three days earlier, I waited for a response.

"Hello? Who is calling?" the secretary asked pleasantly.

"This is Steve Sarkela," I replied. "I have a meeting with Agent Nathan Hawthorne."

"One moment please."

A few seconds later, I heard a click and the door unlocked. As I walked in, I heard the security door shut tight with a clink that was now familiar to me. It was even comforting. Once inside, I followed the same routine to reach the lobby.

Looking at me, the receptionist said, "Agent Hawthorne will be right with you."

Not having to wait long, Agent Hawthorne entered the room. Extending his hand, he said, "Hey Steve!" Asking me to follow him, he led me to the same interrogation room as before where another agent was waiting. After being introduced, we sat down and I played Shamus' recorded message for them. Once they heard it, Agent Hawthorne saved the recording on his computer. Then, we went over the whole ordeal again, from the beginning all the way to the end. They asked about parts of my story repeatedly—to verify exactly what happened. They quizzed me about everything, down to the smallest detail.

While this was happening, Shamus unexpectedly called. Seeing his name pop up on my iPhone, the agents scrambled to get the recording equipment set up before I answered. After starting the recorder, while making sure to save the previous call, they signaled for me to answer.

"Hello?"

"Steve, this is Shamus!"

"What do you ..." I started to say, but Shamus cut me off.

"The attorney canceled the closing." Shamus informed me. "Now you need to set up another closing with another lawyer. This time, we will go together, so I can get my money. Do you understand?"

"Yes."

"I want that money right away!" Shamus demanded.

"Okay, I'll call another lawyer and set it up."

"Set the closing for this afternoon. You hear me! Call me back with the time and place or what happened to you at the house will be nothing compared to what will be coming next!"

Without waiting for me to respond, Shamus hung up. Despite being in FBI headquarters, being thoroughly intimidated, I was shaking badly.

To help calm me down, Agent Hawthorne said, "We are going to get this guy, Steve. You did great on the call but we need to keep going—to fight this through to the end. We are in this with you. We'll get him."

With this, Agent Hawthorne took the reins and started making calls to find a new attorney for the second closing. We spent the next few minutes scheduling a closing for the condo.

Looking at me, Agent Hawthorne said, "We need your phone records, Steve. Can you give me your phone, so our tech guy can download your data into our system?"

Without hesitation, I handed my iPhone to him.

"We are going to tap your phone and record all of your calls and text messages—both incoming and outgoing," he said. Will you sign a release so we don't have to get a warrant?"

"Of course I'll sign," I replied, adding my signature to the document immediately. I added, "If you need my phone records, I can just give you my password. It will save you some time and paperwork."

"You'd do that for us?" Agent Hawthorne replied—surprised by my willingness to help.

"Sure, here it is," I said, writing down the pass code and handing it to him.

Next, he asked, "Did you bring the corporate records for Pelican Gulf, LLC?"

"Yes," I said. Excusing myself to go to the lobby, I retrieved a huge box of records—everything from start to finish on the project. Re-entering the interrogation room, I plopped the box onto the table. Seeing how extensive and detailed my records were, they brought in an accounting specialist, which necessitated us moving out of the interrogation room and into a conference room that had a much larger table.

When they opened the box of records, they had numerous questions for me. "When did you start this company?" They asked. "Did you file taxes? Where are the tax returns? Did you make money? How much money did you make?"

My answer was the same for each question. "Everything is in the box."

They started spreading the contents out on the table like it was a treasure.

"Who is your corporate attorney?"

"Duffy Tipton," I replied, providing them with his contact information.

While answering their questions, my phone rang again. It was Shamus. After the recording devise was connected, I answered, "Hello."

Changing the plans, Shamus ordered, "If you know what's good for you, you'd better bring the money to Ruby Tuesday's at noon tomorrow. Do you hear me?"

"Yes," I replied weakly.

"I want the cash, now! No more closing! Come alone with the money or you and your family are done for."

Not knowing what to say or do, I looked at Agent Hawthorne for direction. He was scribbling fast on a notepad, while at the same time, nodding his head for me to say, "Yes."

"Okay, Shamus," I replied meekly. "I'll be there."

With that, Shamus and I confirmed our meeting for noon at Ruby Tuesday's on James Island.

Having made the appointment, the FBI put everything into full gear. A violent criminal was about to commit a crime right before their eyes, providing them with what they craved more than anything—adventure. Although none of the agents used the word, I knew I was about to participate in a sting.

Chapter 22

Seamless Preparation

A lthough no expert on their procedures, after spending nearly two full days at FBI headquarters, I believe I could have described their office culture pretty well. It was professional and methodical. Although the agents always seemed to be on the go, once the possibility of an agency sting eventuated, the pace picked up considerably.

The difference between before and after was palpable. Excitement was in the air. It was so thick you could cut it with a proverbial knife. To accomplish what they intended to do, I needed to play the leading role in the impending drama. As emotionally rocked as I was at the time, both physically and emotionally, this was a tall order for me and Agent Hawthorne knew it.

Taking me aside, he sat me down to explain the situation. Providing full disclosure, he said, "Steve, we can arrest Shamus right now—Otto too—and this can be over. But if you agree to do what we are planning to do, we can get these criminals locked up for a long time. They will do hard time in a federal prison for their crimes."

Allowing that to sink in, he added, "We will do everything possible to keep you safe during the operation. I promise."

When Agent Hawthorne explained the situation to me this way, I felt pretty sure this was what I wanted to do. My anxiety about having to face Shamus, on the other hand, went straight through the roof. Having nearly been murdered by him and his ongoing threat to kill my family, I wanted Shamus and Otto to be out of my life forever—more than anything else. Because spending years in a federal prison would accomplish that goal, I agreed to do whatever they asked me to do knowing this was clearly my best option. Nevertheless, my resolve wasn't as solid as it needed to be.

Once I agreed, Agent Hawthorne explained there could be some personal risk involved. He said, "Anything can happen at the meeting with Shamus," which certainly wasn't very reassuring. Seeing the anxiety written all over my face, but not wanting to be a pushy salesman, Hawthorne provided me with full disclosure about the entire operation. He explained that it would be dangerous and there was a chance that things could go poorly. At one point, he said, "You could get killed."

This obviously got my attention, but I still wanted to go through with the sting knowing my life would never have value again—not with Shamus on the loose and gunning for me. Seeing how distressed I had become thinking about "the downside," Hawthorne reiterated that this was a completely voluntary operation. I didn't have to meet Shamus at all. He made this very clear.

"There are risks here, Steve," he said. "We may not be able to protect you from those who might be with him."

Perhaps this should have given me pause, but I had already passed the point of no return. Although I was afraid of what Shamus and Otto could do to me—terrified really—I was also mad. Besides, I didn't want to let them get away with it—as my mother had suggested. I wanted those two scoundrels to pay for their crimes and if putting my life at risk was what was needed to make that happen, then so be it.

Not long afterwards, three other agents entered the room, sat down and started preparing me for my meeting with Shamus.

I had assumed this would be a simple, cut and dried operation, but it wasn't. The FBI's planning was precise. They spent hours training me about what to say and what not to say.

One agent stated, "We will have a recording system running. It will record everything during the operation so you need to be careful about what you say, even after you obtain a confession."

Looking at him, I nodded my head that I understood, but he wanted to make sure.

Reiterating how important this was, he added, "No celebrating. No threatening. No bad language. Is that clear?"

"Perfectly," I replied.

"This recording will be used in court. We need you to get Shamus to confess to what he did to you at his house. We want to confirm his previous threats on the recording."

Changing the direction somewhat, the agent placed a map on the table for all of us to see. They had drawn out everything that would happen at Ruby Tuesday—down to the smallest detail. Reviewing it, which we did numerous times, I was very impressed at how well put together the operation was.

Looking up from the map, the agent said, "When you drive into Ruby Tuesday, you need to park in this parking space, Steve—the one right in front of this window."

I nodded my head that I understood.

Again pointing at the map, he said, "We will be parked on the other side of the parking lot watching you."

Seeing that my fear and apprehension was getting the better of me, which I couldn't help, he stopped for a minute to allow me time to settle down. Internally, I was terrified; despite knowing how many FBI agents were involved.

Knowing me better than the others, Agent Hawthorne asked, "Are you okay, Steve?"

I wasn't. I felt sick, scared and nauseous. I was nearing panic, which quickly became apparent to everyone.

Looking at me with deep concern, Agent Hawthorne asked, "Will you be able to go through with this?"

Despite being as rattled as I was, I nodded my head that I would be able to do my part.

Reassuring me and knowing how devastating such an attack could be, he affirmed me. "Steve, we will do everything in our power to keep you safe, but there is no way we can guarantee it completely." He added, "We don't know what he is planning or who may be helping him, but we're planning for the worst case scenario. We will have sharpshooters in place—just in case we have to face a deadly situation."

After letting me think about that for a long moment, Agent Hawthorne returned to what he had said earlier. "You don't have to go through with this meeting. We can go pick him up right now. That's an option. Our case might be tough to prove though, especially if they retain high-powered lawyers. Shamus and Otto might get off with a light sentence." Looking at me, he added, "Remember, you were in Shamus' private home—with the two of them ready to testify against *you*. Your only alternative is to go through with this operation."

Again, allowing me time to think about my decision, he concluded. "If you go through with the meeting, we will see, hear and witness Shamus extorting money from you. That will be incredibly powerful in court."

While listening, thoughts of my beating raced through my mind, but it wasn't just my emotions that were wounded. My ribs continued to hurt and I couldn't breathe deeply without discomfort. I thought about Shamus and Otto slapping and punching me, cursing and threatening me and of receiving so many punches to the face from them that I still couldn't open one eye completely. I remembered the terror of being tied to that chair, waiting for them to kill me.

Then I thought about Shamus and Otto hiring a good lawyer and never having to pay for their crimes. I wanted Shamus and

Otto to go down for this and the sting operation was the best way to accomplish my goal. I knew I couldn't let them get away with it. Taking as deep of a breath as I could, I looked at Agent Hawthorne. Steeling myself for the task ahead, I said, "You can count on me. I'm not going to change my mind. I won't back out. I promise."

Returning my glance, Agent Hawthorne nodded his head, but he also looked me straight in the eye. I had his respect. I could tell that I did and that made me feel proud. It also made me feel like a man for the first time since my nightmare began.

———◇———

Now that I was irreversibly onboard, the FBI sting went into high gear. I was no longer a semi-passive onlooker but a vital part of the operation. To make everything work, several things were required. Doing everything requested of me, you could say that I had jumped in with both feet.

I called my bank and asked them to prepare a cashier's check for $160,000, which was the amount I was scheduled to receive from the sale of the condo. Speaking with a woman from the bank I had known for a long time, she heard trepidation in my voice, which I couldn't hide, so she asked me if I was all right. I told her that I was fine, but I wasn't convincing.

Alarmed enough to transfer the call, another woman, who I did not know, came on the line. Introducing herself as the head of the bank's security, she began asking me numerous questions. Seeing that I was getting nowhere with her, Agent Hawthorne got on the line and introduced himself. This got her attention, but she wasn't convinced he was really with the FBI.

Asking her to call the Charleston FBI office and ask for him, Agent Hawthorne disconnected and waited for her to call. Less than a minute later, she did. In the interim, however, the bank had decided not to get involved. This surprised me, but the woman wouldn't budge even though I had adequate funds in my account to cover the check.

After disconnecting, we were forced to go back to the drawing board. Instead of handing Shamus a cashier's check, which he would know was legitimate; I would have to hand him a personal check from my account. That would probably work, but it might also be a red flag for Shamus. With no other choice, giving him my personal check was what we decided to do.

I spent the rest of the day at the FBI office. By the time I was ready to walk out the door, I was exhausted. I never knew these people were so hard working. It seemed like they never slept. They had people working around the clock on cases like mine.

Just before I left to return to my hotel, Agent Hawthorne stopped me. Looking at me very seriously, he said, "Steve, I am sorry, but I will have to keep your gun until the operation is over. You will need to go into Ruby Tuesday unarmed. Just before the meeting tomorrow, you must give me your weapon. I will return it right after we arrest Shamus."

Somehow, I knew this was going to be required. I expected it so I consented immediately. After sleeping with my Glock every night since my attack, it was not going to be easy turning it over to Agent Hawthorne—not even for an hour.

Chapter 23

Taking Them Down

I didn't sleep well the night before the sting. How could I? In fact, I haven't slept well since it happened—not for years. It's not that I didn't need the rest before meeting with Shamus. I did. Once I would drift off, however, I would awaken with a start—frightened and disoriented. Once being fully awake, I would be unable to drift off again for quite a while.

This is a common sleep pattern for those who have experienced significant personal trauma—it's a problem I wouldn't wish on anybody. Sleep deprivation was one of the unexpected consequences of my attack—one neither Shamus nor Otto could have foreseen. Being traumatized the way I was has produced some permanent hidden scars. It's an emotional wound that I suspect may never heal.

Finally abandoning the effort to sleep that night, I went downstairs to the hotel's breakfast room and poured myself a cup of coffee. It was just 6 a.m. and I needed the java. Nothing could have tasted better.

It's funny, but when you have to face a situation where your life is definitely in jeopardy, you cherish simple things like a cup of coffee. Knowing I had to be at FBI headquarters at eight, I drank a second cup, which tasted just as good and then ate a bowl of cereal. I went back to my room, showered, dressed and left for the day.

Although the pain from Otto's blows had begun to diminish, the bruising hadn't. If anything, I looked worse than the evening it happened. Nevertheless, I poured myself a third cup of coffee and drove downtown for my meeting with Agent Hawthorne and the rest of his team.

Upon arrival, I could see that they had everything in place. It was an impressive operation. Despite my fear and apprehension, I was also pretty excited. Being the center of attention for an FBI sting made me feel important—no doubt about it. My emotions vacillated between boyish excitement and true terror. One moment I wanted to run and the next I wanted to strut my stuff a little—not unlike a wide receiver after catching a game-winning touchdown pass. I couldn't do either, though. This was far too serious and too dangerous an operation. I have to admit—it was exciting.

Having gone over the details numerous times the day before, Agent Hawthorne simply provided me with the "cliff notes" version that morning knowing our time for preparation was short. His instructions were brief and to the point.

While he was talking to me, another agent wired me with a recording device so small it couldn't be detected. After checking to make sure it was operating correctly, we headed out.

Two FBI cars led the way. Another followed behind me. I felt as important as the president of the United States, knowing they received similar treatment from the Secret Service.

Arriving on James Island, we drove past Ruby Tuesday to a vacant parking lot about a mile further down Folly Road. Getting out of their cars, the FBI agents proceeded to put on their bulletproof vests while checking to make sure their weapons were loaded and ready to fire—just in case they were needed.

Watching them do this, I can't even describe to you how it made me feel. It was awe-inspiring and also frightening. The reality of how serious and dangerous this matter was hit me then. It's not something I would recommend putting on your bucket list.

Watching the agents lock and load their weapons made me feel naked. I was the only one who wasn't packing heat. Having had to surrender my Glock to Agent Hawthorne just before we left FBI headquarters, I felt defenseless. It also made my safety completely dependent on them. In one sense, this should have been fine, but I didn't feel good walking into Ruby Tuesday unarmed. Having been thoroughly intimidated by Shamus, I was frightened of being in his presence again.

When everything was ready to go, the FBI gave me some final instructions, which were clear and specific. They told me to go inside the restaurant and not to hold our meeting outside. Most importantly, they told me not to get into Shamus' car under any circumstances.

Then, the agents gave me a very discreet external recorder. In fact, it didn't look anything like a recording device, but it augmented the wire I was already wearing. The agents provided me with specific instructions on how to use it. They told me to place it on the table and not look at it or adjust it in any way. Being crystal clear, the agent said, "Just set it down and start the meeting."

Seeing how nervous I had become, Agent Hawthorne asked, "Are you okay?" He asked me to put out my hand, which I did. Taking hold of it, he said he wanted to feel my pulse to see exactly how stressed out I was. Dropping my hand a few seconds later, he asked me several other questions—all to determine if I was capable of going through with the operation.

"Don't worry," I said with a smile. "I'm ready. Let's do this."

Returning my smile, he nodded, indicating we were all set to go.

Getting in my car a few minutes later, I headed out toward Ruby Tuesday. With my heart racing and my hands tingling, everything felt surreal. Although the drive to the restaurant was very short, it felt like an eternity to get there.

Pulling into Ruby Tuesday's parking lot, I saw Shamus waiting for me in his car, which was parked a ways off. I didn't make eye contact with him or acknowledge that I had even seen his car. Doing as I had been instructed, I pulled my car into the exact space the agents had instructed me to park. Then, still not looking toward Shamus or acknowledging his presence, I began to walk into the restaurant.

Seeing me, Shamus began honking his horn, but I ignored him and walked straight into Ruby Tuesday's instead. Greeting the hostess, she led me to a table where I waited for Shamus. Just as soon as I sat down, I placed the recording device on the table as the agent had instructed. Since Shamus had not yet come inside, I looked around the restaurant casually. I wanted to see if I could spot any of the clandestine agents, hoping I might recognize one or two of them, but I didn't.

Thinking about having to eat with Shamus made my stomach feel queasy, which I hadn't anticipated. The last thing I needed was to get sick to my stomach and have to race to the men's room and vomit. Fighting back the urge, I calmed myself for what was about to happen. I had no choice. Besides, Agent Hawthorne told me there would be fifteen agents there ready to protect me if anything went wrong.

A moment later, Shamus entered the restaurant and looked around. After making eye contact with me, he walked over to the table but he didn't sit down.

Instead, standing over me, he commanded. "Come with me, Steve. We'll talk in my car."

Having been prepared for this, I said emphatically, "No, we'll do business right here or we won't do it at all." Being very firm, I motioned for him to take a seat. There was no way I was going to get in his car and let myself be under his control again.

He was surprised by my insistence, and annoyed, but I held my ground. I could tell he was thinking about it for a moment, tossing the idea around before his greed finally trumped his need to be in complete control.

Conceding to my demand, he took his seat.

"Fine," he said, as he sat down.

I felt a twinge of pride at having been victorious over Shamus in our initial salvo, but it was a small victory. I needed a much more substantive triumph than this. While he was scooting into his seat, I moved the recording device discreetly—just to make sure it captured our conversation. I set it right in the middle of the table. I did this so quickly that Shamus, who was still situating himself in the booth, had no idea what I had just done.

Finally seated and looking directly at me, Shamus' eyes narrowed. In an obvious attempt to bully me, having difficulty hiding his anger, he commanded, "I need you to give me the money."

Responding, I asked, "If I give you the money, how do I know I'll be safe? How do I know you won't try this again?"

Shamus didn't respond. Instead, he continued to bore a hole through me with his intimidating, menacing stare.

Since he wouldn't answer, I continued asking him questions. "What you did at the house with Otto, the way you tortured and beat me, how do I know that will never happen again?"

Doing as I had been instructed, I tried to get a confession from him. We needed it to be on the record.

Finally responding, Shamus said, "No, just give me the money and everything will be okay."

When I heard this, I started to feel intense fury coming from deep within me. Looking him straight in the eye, I said, "You've made me very angry."

When he heard this, I was surprised by his response. Instead of continuing to be confrontational, which I had anticipated, he cowered away—just a little. It looked like he was going to get up and leave, which was the last thing I wanted him to do.

Fearing I might scare him off, I suspected I might have displayed too much antagonism, so I backed off a little. "Where is Otto?" I asked. "I'm scared of him. How do I know he won't come back and kill me?"

Not answering any of my questions directly, which I needed him to verbalize, Shamus replied, "Just give me the money and everything will be okay."

Sneering at him contemptuously, I countered. "You know I don't owe you any money, right? Ahab owes you, not me."

"Yeah, I know," Shamus admitted. "Just write the check and I'll help you get the money back from Ahab."

Taking out my checkbook, I wrote him a check for $160,000. A moment later, I handed it to him.

Taking it from me with a victorious smile on his face, Shamus said, "This will do for now, but if you want to stay safe, you need to give me $40,000 more. I found out you have money in the bank, Steve. Lots of money."

Knowing I would do as he had instructed, I wrote another check for $40,000.

Having concluded our business without bothering to order any food, Shamus stood up and walked out of Ruby Tuesday with my checks in his possession. As soon as he was out the door, two agents, who I had assumed were customers, ran over to me and introduced themselves, flashing their badges.

"Are you all right?" they asked. Smiling, one agent said, "You did great, Steve. The recording is off now, so you can relax and calm down."

Two others agents, who had been drinking martinis at the bar—a young man and a pretty young woman—who looked like a couple on a date, opened their jackets. Flashing their badges and their guns, they ran outside after Shamus while other agents outside were doing the same thing.

Halfway to his car, five agents surrounded Shamus with their guns pointed at his head.

"Freeze!" The lead agent demanded, "Put your hands on your head slowly and don't move!"

Stunned, Shamus didn't move as agents closed in on him from every direction. Doing as he had been directed, Shamus raised his hands and surrendered without incident.

Walking up from behind, one of the agents took Shamus' hands down and handcuffed him. Watching this event unfold through the window of the restaurant made me feel very good. Once Shamus was in handcuffs and knowing he was no longer a threat, I took a deep breath—my first sigh of relief since my beating.

Wisely, one of the agents had suggested that I watch the arrest, telling me it might help me heal from having been violated.

Wondering what was going on, one customer tried to approach me, but he was asked to return to his seat. While the arrest was happening, the restaurant was locked down with agents standing guard at the door. Nobody was allowed in or out. Being the center of attention, all eyes were on me. This was definitely my fifteen minutes of fame, but I was too nervous to enjoy it.

A moment later, indignantly, the manager came over demanding to know what was happening. "I am losing business," he snapped, "and customers want to leave."

Dismissing his pique and providing him with no explanation whatsoever, one agent retorted, "You'll just have to wait. This will be over soon."

Once my arch-nemesis was in handcuffs, I watched as the FBI opened Shamus' car and searched it thoroughly. They found a folder with copies of everything I had in my wallet—credit cards, license, voter ID card, insurance cards and many other personal items.

While they were doing this, another FBI team simultaneously entered Shamus O'Dunnigan's house and did a full criminal investigation. This included vacuuming the house with a special vacuum cleaner—one that collected evidence of a crime. They also used special lights and chemicals to show foot prints, handprints, blood, hair, spit—everything.

Hitting the jackpot, they found the serrated knife Shamus and Otto had used in the crime, along with the duct tape they had used to tie me up. They even found the spit on the wall adjacent to the chair in the room at the end of that long corridor.

After receiving a call, one of the agents said, "We've got it all." Smiling, he added, "and it's just where you said it would be, Steve."

Obviously, the FBI was very pleased with the evidence thay had already obtained, but they were not finished. Digging through the trash, they found the agreements Shamus had drafted and thrown away. They took information from his computer and printer, which showed documents of Shamus providing wiring instructions to the closing attorney.

He wanted the money extorted from me to be deposited into a joint account he had with Ahab. When I learned this, I thought about all the papers I had been forced to sign. Would they also have been transferred to the company jointly owned by Shamus and Ahab?

As you can imagine, this made me wonder how involved my stepfather had been in all of this. Too involved, I suspected. Obviously, such thoughts were very familiar and equally disturbing as I had experienced similar betrayals before. Being devious and deceptive was the Dimesdale way. Perhaps this was another example of it—one accomplished through proxy.

Once the arrest was complete and Shamus was taken off to jail, I was escorted back to the office by two FBI vehicles. With the operation complete, Agent Hawthorne returned my weapon, but he also instructed me to be careful.

"Remember," he said, "Otto has not been apprehended."

This was a warning that was unnecessary. My awareness that Otto Z. Roddick was still at large consumed every fiber of my being. I was terrified that he might find me and exact a terrible revenge. Until he was behind bars, my Glock would remain closer to me than my shadow.

Chapter 24

Holding My Tongue

Unbeknownst to either the FBI or me, during this sting operation, Otto was sitting across the street just off of Folly Road in the parking lot of a strip mall watching the entire event. He was there to keep an eye on things—just in case his partner in crime needed his muscle to seal the deal or to restore order.

Realizing the Federal Bureau of Investigation was involved, which was evident by the blue jackets several of the agents wore and sporting their logo in bold yellow, Otto was just as surprised to see them as Shamus had been. Counting four agents and knowing there were many others unseen, Otto knew better than to try and intervene. Watching them arrest Shamus scared Otto. It let him know he would be next. This frightened the European Karate Champion so much that he nearly wet his pants while observing events unfold from the safety of his car.

Having taken care of the police the night of the attack, neither expected me to go to the FBI. They had never even considered such an eventuality. Choosing discretion over foolishly intervening, knowing he was now a wanted man and a fugitive at large— Otto wisely vacated the area. Acting exactly like a shopper on his way home from the store, he started his car, put it in gear and slowly left the parking lot. Turning right, he headed to I-95, which wasn't far away. Leaving everything behind, knowing not to return to his apartment or place of business, his only goal was to get out of South Carolina as fast as he could—never to return.

Being a fugitive, he knew he had to be careful, but that wasn't going to be easy—not as angry and rattled as he was. Furious he had missed his payday from Shamus, which he anticipated from funds extorted from me, Otto realized they had not only misjudged me—they had overplayed their hand.

Watching Shamus being placed in a police vehicle with his hands cuffed behind him, Otto's goal was to avoid the same fate, if he could help it. Knowing that he and Shamus had won the battle but had lost the war infuriated Otto. I had outsmarted them and they never saw it coming.

Biting his lip, Otto wished he had finished me off. That would have been a far better outcome, which Otto now realized. Despite the disaster he had just witnessed, at least he was free and he intended to stay that way. Nevertheless, he still had one piece of unfinished business left to do. When that was completed, he would disappear forever.

◇

Once Shamus was in custody, we returned to FBI headquarters where my Glock was returned to me. Like forgetting to put on your watch or a favorite piece of jewelry, I felt naked without it, but that wasn't the worst part of it. I also felt unsafe. It's a feeling I have had ever since my attack. Having my weapon nearby is the norm for me now and I suspect that will never change.

After leaving FBI headquarters, I didn't go back to the hotel. Instead, I chose to return to my daughter's home, which I considered to be a much safer place to stay. Although the FBI had an "All Points Bulletin" out for the arrest of Otto Z. Roddick, having already searched every place the karate champion frequented, the authorities still hadn't located him. He remained at large.

That night, I slept fitfully, constantly fearful that Otto would show up and murder me along with the rest of my family, but that didn't happen. I was nervous that Shamus would somehow find a way to contact Otto and the two of them would be able to plot further mayhem against me. Perhaps my thoughts were irrational, but I couldn't stop them from racing through my mind. Instead of basking in the victory I had achieved over Shamus, the looming threat from his partner consumed my attention. Instead of feeling victorious, which was my right, I was consumed with dread and foreboding.

The following day though, I received a call from Agent Hawthorne telling me that two U.S. Marshals discovered Otto's car in a rest area just outside of Palm Beach, Florida, where I lived. Confronting him, when he came out of the men's room, Otto refused to be subdued easily. Resisting arrest, he foolishly believed he could overpower two trained officers of the law who had already called for backup.

Pummeling Otto, Shamus' partner was thrown to the ground where an officer's knee was placed on his back. Forcing his hands behind him, Otto was handcuffed, put in a police car and led off to the Palm Beach County jail. He would stay there for three months before being returned to South Carolina to stand trial for kidnapping, aggravated assault and extortion.

Learning that Otto had been arrested relieved me, but hearing that his apprehension occurred in the town where I lived made me think I wasn't irrationally fearful about being targeted for revenge. If he weren't in Palm Beach looking for me, then why would he go there in the first place? Even a dolt like Otto must have realized that the authorities would be looking for him in South Florida. Although relieved Otto was in custody, discovering where he had been arrested was unnerving.

Once Otto was in cuffs, the imminent danger that had consumed my consciousness was over. That part of my nightmare was finished, but it was just act one of the looming drama. Act two, which involved dealing with public reaction, my long-term recovery from assault and the trial, was about to commence—beginning the very next day.

The attack on me became a major news story in the area, as one article after another was printed. It easily made the local news shows, but the stories being reported were much different than what really happened. Essentially, there was disbelief that either Shamus O'Dunnigan or Otto Z. Roddick was capable of perpetrating such a heinous crime. People simply didn't believe it was true—lots of them, including nearly everybody from my family.

When I realized this, it was not only surprising, but it also became infuriating. I was completely appalled by how distorted the news coverage had been. Knowing I would feel this way, especially after reading one particularly erroneous account of events, Agent Hawthorne gave me a call.

After greeting one another and congratulating each other over our success, Hawthorne said, "Steve, I know how galling the latest newspaper story was for you, but I want to caution you about making any public statements."

"But the papers have everything wrong," I countered. "They are actually making me look like the bad guy. Shouldn't I set the record straight?" I protested.

"No, you shouldn't, Steve." Agent Hawthorne said emphatically. "In fact, it's essential that you refrain from responding at all."

"Why?" I asked.

"Because it could hurt our court case, that's why. In 'setting the record straight,' you might say something inadvertently that some sleazy lawyer could twist against us. I've seen it happen many times," he explained firmly.

Since I didn't respond for quite a while, Agent Hawthorne knew he hadn't convinced me. Making another appeal, he asked, "What is our goal here, Steve?"

"To send them to prison," I responded without equivocation.

"Exactly," he concurred. "Then, anything you might do to hinder our goal wouldn't be a good thing, would it?"

"No," I admitted, reluctantly accepting the wisdom of his logic. Doing so was difficult though. Everything in me wanted to speak out boldly, to shout out the truth publicly—just like I am telling you now. Remaining silent, regardless of how wise it was, went against the grain of my character. I wanted to expose their deeds of darkness.

Knowing this was exactly how I felt, Agent Hawthorne, who had become my friend, encouraged me by reminding me of the gratification I would receive if I stayed quiet and won the cases against them. It would be well worth the wait to set the record straight. Accepting his assessment as true, there was nothing left for me to do in South Carolina and I knew it. Disconnecting, I knew my mini-vacation from hell was coming to an end.

One afternoon, I received a call from the federal judge presiding over the case against Shamus O'Dunnigan. The judge was going to set Shamus' bond at $100,000. After listening to what I had to say, which Shamus and his lawyer could hear, since I was on speakerphone, the judge upped the bail to $200,000. I had hoped the judge would remand Shamus, but he didn't. Nevertheless, I was assured Shamus would have no contact with me—not if he wanted to stay out of jail until the trial.

A few days later, after saying goodbye to my daughter and her family, Daniel and I got back into my BMW and headed back to the Sunshine State. While passing through Georgia, as I thought about all that had happened, I realized there would be no good reason to return to South Carolina until the trial.

I assumed this would happen fairly quickly, but I was mistaken. It required several years, which meant my life hung in limbo for a long time.

Chapter 25

The Wheels of Justice Move Slowly

'''ve heard it said that the wheels of justice move slowly, but from my perspective, they barely moved at all. At least this is how I felt—especially with the trial constantly hanging over my head. From one of my history classes in high school, I remembered learning that people accused of a crime have the right to a "speedy trial," but this certainly wasn't what was happening—not in the cases against Shamus O'Dunnigan and Otto Z. Roddick.

Although I wanted it over with, they wanted to postpone it for as long as possible. By stringing it out, they would remain free on bail. While they were enjoying life, I was distraught, completely caught up in my emotional prison.

I was a psychological mess from the crime—no doubt about it. The stress from it might have proven to be too much for me, but there were two factors that were instrumental in helping me survive. The first was my counselor, Dwight Long. Dwight, who was a former CIA agent, experienced the same kind of trauma I did. One day, a deranged maniac came into his office and killed several people by spraying CIA headquarters with gunfire. Dwight, having narrowly missed being killed, became a victim nonetheless.

Once the ordeal was over, Dwight never returned to his duties with the CIA. Instead, after going back to school for a graduate degree, he began counseling survivors of attacks—just like the one I experienced. Because he understood exactly how I felt, having survived a similar experience, Dwight became instrumental in helping me maintain my sanity. Without his support, understanding and consistent encouragement, I suspect I might have gone off the deep end. That's how disturbed I became after having suffered a life-altering traumatic experience inflicted by Shamus and Otto.

Dwight helped me cover the downside of my debilitating trauma, but there was another person who gave me hope for the future and a reason to live—my future wife, Lillemor. Although I met her before the actual attack happened, falling in love with her instantly, her strength became vital to my survival after my attack—more than any other factor. Without her love and support, I definitely wouldn't have made it through the trial as a sane person. It wasn't that she became my crutch, helping me to deal with my stressful situation. It was more than that. She became my anchor—someone solid to hold onto, to keep me from falling flat on my face. She is my true soul mate and provided me with the right amount of support, whenever and wherever I needed it.

Never rejecting me because of my emotional wounding, Lillemor became my emotional rock—the first woman I have ever been able to count on in my entire life, without betraying me. Always supportive and never threatening, I knew Lillemor would stay and never leave. Without her by my side, I felt certain the weight of the impending trial would have been more than I could have ever endured on my own.

Like me, Lillemor was an Apostolic Lutheran. I met her at our denominational conventions in Minnesota. She was the real deal and once she was in my life, we bonded instantly.

Deciding to marry six months after the attack, we went to the courthouse in Palm County and became legally married, which was necessary because Lillemor was a citizen of Finland. By marrying a U. S. citizen in Florida, it helped her immigration status. Our goal was for her to become an American—an objective that has been fulfilled.

Our "real wedding" occurred the following July in Finland and it was wonderful. My brother, Rodney, and his family came to support me. Although I was concerned that Lillemor's family wouldn't like me and consider me to be damaged goods, my apprehensions were groundless. All of them were very nice and thoroughly supportive.

Once married, we flew to Milan and enjoyed a wonderful honeymoon, except for being preoccupied and apprehensive about Shamus or Otto showing up. Fear of another confrontation with them, although groundless, followed me wherever I went. Essentially, my internal terror became my shadow—always with me, no matter what.

After our honeymoon in Northern Italy, where I ate gelato four times a day, we returned to South Florida and have remained there ever since. I continued to work for my brother while Lillemor developed her own business as an accountant. If she had been around years earlier when I first got involved with Ahab's shady deal, I doubt I would have ever gotten into the mess I have had to deal with.

Leaving her family and lifestyle behind in Finland was very difficult for her at first, but she has adjusted magnificently. With her around, my life stabilized and became more normal each day. With a true partner in life, my decision-making skills have improved immensely. Nevertheless, my struggles with post-traumatic stress continue. They will always be there, but they are getting better—one day at a time.

Despite everything coming together nicely for Lillemor and me, like a tropical storm, the dark cloud of the trial for Shamus and Otto continued to loom over me. I was unable to fully relax, enjoy life or be carefree. As each week passed, the trial moved closer. I feared the destruction it might bring with it, including potential bodily harm.

In early May 2012, two years after the attack, Leland Girard, the Assistant U.S. Attorney, called to go over our case. During the call, which lasted quite a while, he was thorough, detailed and kind, filling me in on exactly what was happening.

"I'd like to clarify how this process works, Steve," Girard explained. Talking about the disposition of the charges, he added, "This case is going to go one of two ways. It could go to a full trial with a jury, or they could ask for a plea bargain."

Being confused by what that might entail, he enlightened me about how a plea bargain works. "More often than not, in a case like this, they will ask for a plea bargain. Because our evidence is very strong, they probably will. Plea bargains are more like business deals than anything else. This would work for the defense because it would guarantee a lighter sentence. Would you be willing to accept a plea bargain?"

Thinking about it, I replied, "Yes, but only if they remain in prison for a long time."

Clarifying how a plea bargain works in sentencing, Girard added, "There are federal guidelines for crimes like this one. For example, Shamus O'Dunnigan is being charged with six different felonies. Each one carries a sentence of between three-to-seven years—the maximum being nine, with the minimum being three years for each count."

Nodding my head that I understood, Girard asked, "Would you be okay making a deal for five years per count?"

Being very candid, I replied, "No, absolutely not. It needs to be at least seven years."

"Okay," Girard replied. "I'll keep that in mind."

Being assured we had a strong case and were in the driver's seat, he disconnected shortly thereafter.

In late May, I flew to Charleston, South Carolina, for the upcoming trial of Shamus O'Dunnigan and Otto Z. Roddick. Despite all of the impressive evidence the FBI had amassed, as the victim, I was still the most important part of the case. Upon arrival, we went through everything that happened, laboring over each piece of evidence to make sure we were completely in sync. It was a grueling and exhaustive process.

Meeting again the following day, Girard's assistant, Robert Leland, sat down with me. During this meeting, the two attorneys laid out our situation.

Speaking first, Leland said, "This is how the process is going to work. It takes a lot of time and patience to succeed in court. It's like a chess game."

Understanding his analogy, I nodded my head that I was following and asked him to proceed, which he did.

"These guys have good lawyers and they are going to try to wiggle free using anything they can come up with, but we're not going to let them. We're not going to let them be successful with it anyway."

I liked the way Leland was heading and, with a smile on my face, told him so.

Returning my smile, without losing his train of thought, he continued. "We have these guys locked down with solid evidence, but we can't make any mistakes." Looking at me, he added, "So, we have to go over everything in detail, okay?"

"Absolutely," I affirmed. "Whatever it takes to put these guys away."

Both prosecutors nodded affirmatively. Leland pulled out his briefcase. Looking at me, he asked, "Then let's get started, shall we?"

We spent the next four hours going over hundreds of photos of the crime scene, sorting out the best ones to be used for the trial. Once our selections were finalized, Leland suggested that they test me—just to determine my emotional strength for what was about to happen. They did this by playing out various courtroom scenes, asking me one penetrating question after the other—all designed to rattle me instead of obtaining information.

Girard explained that the defense could question the prime witness about anything concerning the case. He warned that they would have no mercy. This meant I had to be strong. To try and prevent me from being blindsided by an unnerving question, Leland talked me through the entire assault step by step, even using the photos to do so.

Trying to intimidate me—just like Shamus and Otto's attorneys would—Leland bullied me. "Is this where you were when they attacked you?" Next, he showed me a picture of the stairway. "Is this where they used the knife?" When he showed me a picture of the small closet with the big wooden chair they used to tie me up, I started breathing heavily. Unnerved, tears welled up in my eyes and streamed down my cheeks. I couldn't help it.

Nevertheless, I answered the question "Yes. That's the place where it happened!"

Seeing how rattled I had become, Leland suggested we take a break, eat some lunch and continue afterwards. Knowing I had to harden my emotions and become resolute, I made a conscious effort to become tougher. We worked diligently for the rest of the day.

Despite how unnerved I had become, I never resented what was happening knowing that my villains' defense attorneys would be ruthless and aggressive with their treatment. Committed to proving their clients' innocence, despite their obvious guilt, it was the duty of these pettifoggers to exploit any weakness in me they could. To counter them meant our preparation had to be meticulous, thorough and exhausting. Spent but prepared, we were ready for the trial. It was set for July—just a few weeks away.

Chapter 26

Being A Hero

T wo months later in late July, Lillemor and I drove to Charleston for the event I had anticipated and dreaded for so long. The trial of Shamus and Otto was about to commence. Although I had longed for this time—my day for justice—I simultaneously feared it.

Now that it was here, my emotions ran the gambit from jubilation to despair—from hope for the future to an alarming foreboding. I wanted to stand and fight one minute and run away the next. Hoping for victory, while fearing that everything might go terribly wrong, I was an emotional basket case.

Recognizing this, Lillemor became my pillar, helping me stand my ground. She became my source of strength, repeatedly showing tender mercies that undergirded me, especially when I became fearful, weak and apprehensive. My hope was the trial would provide me with closure. Nevertheless, dreading what was about to transpire exacerbated my fears and apprehensions. Despite overwhelming and conflicting emotions, my commitment to go through with the trial never wavered. I had come too far to quit before my goal was achieved.

Although I certainly didn't feel like a hero—being so scared that I didn't even have spit in my mouth—my wife assured me that I was behaving heroically.

She affirmed me by saying, "There's nothing wrong with being scared, Steve. I'm scared too. That's not what makes a man a hero. It's what you do that counts—not how you feel about it at the time."

Looking at me, she added, "Being a hero is doing the right thing regardless of the consequences, despite your fears. That's what makes a man a hero."

After affirming me like this repeatedly, she would frequently take my hand and pray for me to have strength—sometimes in English, while at other times she prayed in Swedish. You can't imagine how much her validations meant to me. They always seemed to come at the precise moment I needed them. While making the long drive north—the same one Daniel and I had made two years earlier—I reflected on Lillemor's affirmations repeatedly. They were like manna from heaven.

We arrived in Charleston on July 21. That afternoon, I met with Dean Girard, the prosecutor. He informed me that Shamus O'Dunnigan had admitted everything and had made the decision to plead guilty to his crimes in open court the following day. This meant Shamus was taking the plea bargain that had been offered.

This surprised me. I felt certain he would fight until the bitter end, but when push came to shove, he folded like a cheap card table.

With Shamus accepting the plea bargain, which spared me from having to testify against him, this meant that one of the villains was down. Unfortunately, there was another remaining. Otto had not yet accepted his plea bargain, but his lawyers were still trying to negotiate a deal for him—similar to the one Shamus had just accepted.

Not knowing if there was going to be a trial for Otto or not, we still needed to prepare for the trial—just in case. This meant we had to work throughout the weekend, preparing for the Monday morning trial. I was surprised by how diligently the prosecutors worked, especially since I thought we had already gone over the material so many times.

When I mentioned how surprised I was that Shamus had accepted a plea bargain, Girard said he wasn't surprised at all. He told me Shamus looked very ill. Tired and broken, the stress of his impending trial had worn Shamus down considerably. Two years of steady pressure had taken its toll on him, according to Girard.

When Girard said this, it made me feel funny. Despite being on opposite sides, I understood exactly how Shamus felt. It was eerie, but in some ways, I actually identified with him, having experienced the same debilitating stress for so long.

Shamus looked so unhealthy, according to Girard, that he suspected my attacker would die in prison. Knowing I would never have complete peace while Shamus remained alive, this was just fine with me. Girard added that Shamus was taking pills for numerous medical problems, including high blood pressure, manic-depression, anxiety, attention deficit disorder and a life-threatening heart disease. Since all of Shamus' crimes were violent, making them "Class A" felonies, his time in prison would probably exceed his life expectancy by many years.

Later, the prosecutors showed me the evidence that would be used in court. They told me I would be asked to identify the knife and scissors. We went through numerous photos of the house and crime scene again, which was particularly brutal for me to revisit. They had photos of everything—the broken glass, the tape used to tie me up, the chair and hundreds of other things.

Although we were preparing for trial, we also felt pretty certain a plea bargain would be reached with Otto—one that would allow him to stay in the United States after serving his time in prison. This is how we felt Sunday afternoon, the day before Otto's trial was scheduled to begin. Our thinking was that

with any luck, the plea bargain would be reached and it would
all be over.

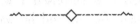

Bright and early the following morning, however, Lillemor
and I were awakened with the news that Otto had refused to
accept his final plea bargain offer. That meant his trial was
moving forward. Although this surprised the prosecutors and the
FBI, somehow I knew this was going to happen. It was my
destiny to confront my torturer and I knew it. It was something
I needed to do. Although not looking forward to it, I knew it
was a mountain I needed to climb—a stronghold that needed
to be assaulted.

I didn't have much time to be philosophical, though. We had
to be in court by 9 a.m., which was difficult, but we made it
with one minute to spare. Promptly at 9 a.m., the judge entered
the courtroom and began the proceedings, starting with the case
against Shamus O'Dunnigan.

When I saw Shamus walk into the room to enter his plea
bargain, I felt a cold chill. I also noticed that Girard was right.
Shamus didn't look good. His countenance wasn't intimidating—
at least not to anybody other than me.

Looking at Shamus, the judge asked, "Is anyone forcing you
to plead guilty to these charges?"

"No," Shamus replied, sweating profusely. His hands were
shaking, which let me know how scared he was.

The judge followed his first question by immediately asking,
"Do you plead guilty to all of the charges?"

Instead of answering the question directly, like he was
supposed to do, Shamus looked at his attorney and stammered
something about finding another way to resolve the case. To me,
it seemed like he wanted to back out of his plea bargain and have
a trial, but that's not what his lawyer wanted for him.

Looking at Shamus like he was a complete fool, the lawyer explained in condescending terms that he had to respond, "Yes," to everything. If he didn't, his plea bargain would be discarded and there would be a trial.

After listening to Shamus and his lawyer bicker for a while, the judge intervened. "If you have been promised anything by your lawyer, the prosecuting attorney or anyone else about how many years you would stay in prison, forget about it. This is my courtroom, and I haven't decided what to do with you yet."

With no option other than complete compliance, Shamus capitulated, accepting his fate.

When the judge returned to reading Shamus a long list of conditions regarding his plea bargain—it required fifteen minutes, Shamus admitted his guilt about everything, which was very gratifying. As he left the courtroom—now a convicted felon— Shamus cast a menacing look at me. Not suspecting this would happen, a pang of fear went straight to the core of my being, rattling me badly. Despite this, it was over. Because Shamus' ability to exact retribution on me ceased to be a viable option, I sighed with relief.

Once Shamus was convicted, without taking a break, Otto's trial followed immediately. Taking the floor for our side, prosecuting the case, Girard began.

About an hour later, I was called to testify. Walking to the witness stand, with the judge and jury already seated, I felt knots turning in my stomach. Although we had gone through what would happen numerous times, I still felt stressed beyond words. It was difficult being in the same room with the man who had mercilessly beaten me two years earlier.

Otto's side of the courtroom was filled with people who had come to show their support. Knowing what he had done, this was particularly galling. On my side, there was my wife, my counselor, Agent Hawthorne and a few others—that's all. The difference between the two sides of the courtroom was dramatic.

When the judge asked me to come forward to be sworn in, my heart was pounding and I felt my pulse racing. After committing to tell the truth, I walked over to the witness box beside the judge and sat down.

Just as soon as I was seated, the judge instructed, "Make sure you keep close to the microphone so the court can hear."

Once I was situated, Girard stood up to question me.

Talking to myself, I said, "Just answer his questions—no more, no less." Girard had been very strict about this in preparing me to testify.

"What's your name?" Girard asked.

"Steven Sarkela."

"And how old are you, Steven?"

"I am fifty-one years old."

Girard turned to face the courtroom. With a ubiquitous gesture, he asked, "Do you see the man called 'Otto'—the man who beat you and put a knife to your throat?" Not waiting for me to answer, he continued. "After beating you, he tied you to a chair and continued committing torturous acts against you while still holding a knife to your throat. If you see that man, would you please point him out to the court?"

"Yes, I see him," I said, pointing directly at Otto. "He is sitting right there."

Continuing, Girard asked, "Is this the man who held a knife to your throat while demanding you to call your twelve-year-old son during the night of your abduction on June 3, 2010?"

"Yes, it's the same man," I replied, but my voice had begun to quiver.

Girard walked to his desk, retrieved a box and brought it to me. "Do you recognize anything inside this box?"

I opened the box and started to cry. In it was the same knife Shamus and Otto had used at the house. It looked terrible. How could I ever forget its sharp, serrated edge? "Yes," I replied through my tears.

"Is that the knife they used when they brought you up the stairs?" Girard inquired.

"Yes," I answered, choking back my tears.

Liking the way things were going, Girard brought another box forward. When he handed it to me, I opened it and saw the scissors they had used that night.

"Are these the scissors Shamus and Otto used when they threatened to cut off your testicles?"

"Yes," I replied weakly. By this time though, I was weeping uncontrollably and couldn't continue.

"Stop!" the judge thundered, interrupting the prosecution's questions. "I'm going to give Mr. Sarkela some time to regain his composure."

Placing his hand over his microphone, he leaned over to me and whispered, "Take your time. I know this has been a horrible thing for you to have to remember."

A short while later, after I had calmed down, Girard continued.

Since I hadn't answered the question satisfactorily, Girard pressed the issue. "Alright, Steven, are these the scissors Shamus O'Dunnigan and Otto Roddick used when they threatened to cut off your testicles?"

Although I knew what was coming, my emotions rushed out like a breaking dam and I was unable to speak.

Hammering his gavel, the judge said, "We will be taking a thirty minute recess. Would someone please bring Mr. Sarkela a tissue?"

Looking to my left, where the jury was seated, I saw three women crying. Waiting until nearly everyone had left the courtroom, I rose and walked out with Girard. He encouraged me to keep going, telling me I was doing fine.

"Don't hold back the tears," he exhorted, after the court cleared. "It's okay."

I felt numb. Going through this again was a terrible

nightmare, far worse than I had anticipated, but I had to persevere. There was no other option. Trying to refocus, I remembered that my counselor told me to breathe deeply, so that's exactly what I did.

Returning to the courtroom after the break, I took the witness seat again. Girard resumed his questioning, returning to exactly the place where we left off. When he did, I felt much better and stronger. I knew I would be able to answer his questions without further incident.

Crying did me a great deal of good. It released most of my pent-up, stressful emotions. Girard finished his questions soon thereafter, which meant it was the defense's turn to question me.

This was going to be the difficult part and I knew it—so did everybody else. Otto had hired a big shot lawyer from Miami. When he witnessed my emotional outburst earlier, it was like showing red meat to a hungry wolf. Being convinced he could break me, he came out swinging with both fists.

"What's your name?" he asked contemptuously.

"Steven Sarkela"

"What did you say?" he challenged. "I can't hear you. Is something wrong with your voice? Speak up!"

He was taunting me, being purposefully rude, trying to make me angry, but it didn't work. Instead of being intimidated, I kept my eyes focused on the prosecution table, where my advocates sat. In a non-verbal way, they instilled confidence in me, which really bothered Otto's attorney.

Being confrontational, he asked, "What are you looking at?"

Shifting my gaze from my advocates to stare at him, I calmly replied, "Well, I'm looking at you."

Immediately making eye contact, looking daggers at me, he did his best to break down my defenses. Not allowing him to do so, I smiled, which infuriated him. Seeing that he had failed, he abandoned his strategy and tried a different one. Having won that round, I felt more confident and was ready for his next question.

"Did my client ever explicitly say he would kill you?" Otto's attorney asked.

I had to think about that. Pausing for a moment, I pondered his question.

Unwilling to give me a moment, he snapped "Go on, tell us. Did he?" Otto's attorney pushed me for a quick answer, but I remembered Girard telling me I could take my time answering, so I did.

I couldn't remember Otto specifically saying that he was going to kill me. I never really thought about it, especially since it was Shamus O'Dunnigan that had done almost all of the talking.

Finally responding to the lawyer's question, I slid my index finger across my throat, while saying, "Otto took his finger and made a throat slitting gesture."

"Answer my question," Otto's attorney bellowed, nearly screaming.

I repeated my demonstration, this time moving my finger theatrically, while saying, "He went like this, while Shamus O'Dunnigan was shouting and swearing. 'I will kill you, Otto will kill you!'"

"Just answer my question, yes or no?" Otto's lawyer demanded.

Intervening, the judge said, "He has already shown you, counselor. He made a throat cutting gesture. It meant, 'I will cut your throat.' Move on. Mr. Sarkela made the gesture and this court will recognize this as saying it."

I had won another round and I knew it. By the looks coming from the prosecution table, they knew it too. Despite this, Otto's attorney, knowing his case was slipping away, continued to harass me. He tried to make me angry and emotional, but I foiled him consistently, reminding the jury about the worst parts of the crime with my answers. Seeing that he was making things worse for Otto, his lawyer wrapped up his questions quickly, which was just fine with me.

Once he was finished, it was the prosecutor's turn to continue making the case, which they did. That afternoon, they went through a mountain of evidence obtained from the crime scene requiring the remainder of the day.

Chapter 27

A Just Verdict

On Tuesday, we returned to the courtroom at 9 a.m. I noticed Otto's side wasn't as full as it had been the day before. In fact, it was almost as empty as my side. Perhaps people were just busy, but I suspected they didn't return because of what they had heard the previous day. What really happened was far different than the version Otto had been telling them for two years. My assumption was they had come to believe Otto was the real victim—not me. Seeing so many empty seats was gratifying and provided me with another small, deliciously victorious moment.

The prosecutor, Dean Girard, began calling expert witnesses. The forensic expert established that my fingerprints were all over Shamus' house, including places they shouldn't have been—like the door jam, where I held on for dear life until Shamus put the serrated knife to my throat to subdue me.

A DNA expert was called and she testified that the spit and blood found on the wall in the little room was mine. She said it was a 100 percent match. Looking at the jury, it was obvious this was important to them.

As I thought back to that night, I remembered how difficult it was for me to even get spit in my mouth, as dehydrated as I was, but my plan had worked. If they had killed me—as they had threatened they would numerous times—the blood and spit that was on the wall would have been enough to convict them of my murder. This pleased me even more than Otto's friends abandoning him the second day of the trial.

Building our case methodically, Girard called a local karate expert to testify about Otto's strength and skill. Praising my attacker, the man said it would have been easy for him to subdue an out of shape fifty-year-old man like me. By extolling Otto's proficiency, the witness thought he was helping his friend, but he wasn't. Instead, he was doing the exact opposite, digging a much deeper hole for him.

Seeing how masterfully Girard was developing the case gave me a great deal of confidence. He was a skilled prosecutor—no doubt about it. It was obvious our case was in good hands.

To establish the motive for my attack, Girard called Paige Steiner—the closing attorney for the sale of the condo—to the witness box. When he did, a middle-aged, nervous woman entered the courtroom. After being sworn in, Girard began to question her.

"Can you state your name for the court?" he asked.

"Paige Steiner," she replied, having to pull the microphone closer to be heard.

Proceeding, Girard asked: "Did Shamus O'Dunnigan show up at your office on June 4, 2010, for a closing when you expected Steven Sarkela to be there instead?"

"Yes, Shamus O'Dunnigan came—not Steve," she affirmed.

"Did Shamus O'Dunnigan attempt to receive the proceeds from Steven Sarkela's closing?"

Steiner, speaking in short, choppy sentences, replied, "Yes, he did."

"Did Shamus O'Dunnigan present you with any documents at that time?" Girard asked.

"Yes, he did."

"Are these the documents?" Girard inquired, approaching the witness after gaining permission from the judge.

She examined them and nodded her head. "Yes, they are."

Turning to face the judge, Girard asked, "Your honor, if it pleases the court, the United States government would like to enter these documents into evidence."

"Yes, you may," the judge replied. "Does the defense have any questions for the witness?"

Otto's lawyer stood and said; "No, your honor. No questions."

Once the documents were entered and motive was established, another nail in Otto's coffin had been hammered into place.

Next, Officer Krumpky of the Mount Pleasant Police Department, who was at Shamus' house the night I was attacked, was called to the stand. Spinning his testimony to mitigate his incompetence, the officer stated that the long-sleeve shirt I was wearing on the night in question prevented him from seeing any cuts or bruising. He gave this testimony without knowing the FBI had already entered a photo of my short-sleeved shirt into evidence, which destroyed this cop's tenuous credibility.

Clearly more interested in the architecture of Shamus' house than admitting he had failed to do his duty, the judge dismissed him telling the officer he would make a better PR man than a police officer. This made everybody in the courtroom laugh—everyone other than me. I had hoped there would be some significant negative consequences for the Mount Pleasant Police Department, but there never were. The fact that nothing was done to improve how they handle situations like mine still bothers me to this day.

Adjourning for the day after Officer Krumpky's buffoonish testimony was complete, bright and early the following day, Special Agent Hawthorne was called to the stand. The difference between his testimony and that of the clown from the Mount Pleasant Police Department was like night and day.

Agent Hawthorne began by showing the pertinent phone records, displaying all of the calls originating from Shamus' phone, Otto's phone and my phone on a large TV screen. Each record was color-coded—Shamus' were yellow, Otto's were blue, and mine were green. The display also showed the duration of each call, bolstering my testimony about receiving threatening calls.

Continuing, Agent Hawthorne showed every piece of evidence recovered from Shamus' house. As the entire courtroom watched, Otto's fate was being sealed one step at a time. When Hawthorne was finished with this, he showed the folder Shamus had in his car with my name on it. It contained all kinds of papers, including my driver's license, credit cards, voter's registration card and insurance cards. It even had a love note from Lillemor. I was thankful it had been written in Swedish, which also relieved her.

Agent Hawthorne's televised presentation was followed by his interview with Otto Z. Roddick. Hawthorne explained that Otto had confessed to everything in detail—assaulting me, tying me up and torturing me. It was stated under oath in his plea bargain. His confession would have been off the record if he had passed his lie detector test, which he didn't. Otto failed the polygraph on two separate occasions. This meant his confession was fair game. Being condemned by his own words and having made their case against him, the prosecution rested.

Chomping at the bit, Otto's high-priced Miami lawyer rose to present Otto's defense. As the defense's first witness, Shamus O'Dunnigan was called to the witness stand. Escorted into the courtroom by two guards, Shamus took his seat and began to answer questions. He talked quite a bit about Ahab, including telling the court that Ahab, "his mentor," and Jezzy, had twenty-four children between them, which seemed to tickle everybody. Shamus also bragged about the big deals he and Ahab had made over the years. Finally, Shamus blurted, "Steven Sarkela attacked me at my table while we were making a deal!"

When Shamus said this, it was a contradiction to what he had told the Mount Pleasant Police the evening I was attacked. That night, he told the police he had come home, accompanied by Otto, to discover me robbing his house. What Shamus didn't know was that just before he took the stand, Otto's confession confirmed my story and the FBI's evidence with complete accuracy. Already a convicted felon, Shamus' testimony certainly didn't help Otto.

After the defense was finished with Shamus, it was the prosecution's turn to question him. Showing Shamus a folder titled *Steven Sarkela*, Girard asked, "Have you seen this before?"

"Well, it looks like my handwriting."

Girard projected the contents of the folder onto the large screen. It was full of my personal documents. "Now, why would you need to make copies of these documents and keep them in a folder, Mr. O'Dunnigan?"

"I thought Steve might be moving to Finland," Shamus stammered, "I needed a way to find him, if he did." Obviously, this wasn't credible, but the prosecutor let it go.

Then, the prosecutor instructed an FBI agent to play the recording of Shamus O'Dunnigan making threats to me at Ruby Tuesday and on several telephone conversations. It was amplified for the court to hear.

As Shamus heard himself screaming and swearing through the speakers, his head slumped and he looked disheartened, perhaps even sad. After he heard it, Shamus testified, "I can't believe I was that angry. That sounded real bad," he admitted, showing sorrow—perhaps even remorse—for the first time. For a brief moment, it made him seem human.

A second later, hardening his heart, Shamus looked across the courtroom directly at me. While making eye contact he yelled, "Your mother did this to you, Steve!"

When Shamus said this, it hit me like a ton of bricks. It was the final piece of the puzzle and it had just fallen into place. He confirmed my mother had caused the crime—it was hard for me to even conceptualize such a thing, let alone accept it as being valid. Shamus had just stated that my mother, Jezzy, was deeply involved in the crime—its planning, its execution and its cover-up. Jezzy's goal, co-planned with her husband, was to extort money from me. He was saying she planned to use my money to pay Ahab's one million dollar debt to Shamus O'Dunnigan.

Having been humiliated in open court by the threats he had just heard himself saying, in a moment of complete candor, Shamus spoke the truth and I knew it instantly. His revelation pierced me to the heart and I was unnerved. Until he said what he did, I had never even considered such a possibility—not until Shamus uttered his nerve-shattering words. Who would? What son would ever consider that his mother could be that treacherous, that hateful or that serpentine?

"Your mother did this to you!" Shamus had admitted and his words reverberated in my mind, rattling every fiber of my being. Heartbroken and overwhelmed by powerful emotions, I fled the courtroom, weeping openly. Finding an empty room, I slumped to the ground in agony and wept bitter tears.

With my mind racing, I began to recall every interaction I had had with my mother since the crime—Ahab too. I had often wondered why Jezzy and Ahab had acted so strangely throughout my terrible ordeal, but now I understood. I had complete clarity. They not only skipped being in court to support me, they hadn't even offered me any kind of encouragement. Now, all of that made sense. They couldn't because they were on the other side—in business with my attacker, Shamus O'Dunnigan.

In preparing for the case, I had asked them numerous times to provide me with whatever information they could about Shamus O'Dunnigan. I wanted them to help me prepare for the trial, but they never did. They refused each request by ignoring it. Now, their behavior made perfect sense to me. In the aftermath of the attack, I never received an inquiry about my injuries either. My mother never called, not even after she had been informed about how badly I had been beaten. The only time she did call was to tell me not to press charges against Shamus.

At the time, her call seemed bizarre. Now that I had been enlightened, it made perfect sense. Being behind everything, she just wanted it to go away. She wanted me to be a good little boy and shield her from ever being discovered or from ever being held accountable.

Finally realizing the possibility of what Shamus said nearly made me sick. I had to calm myself down, regain my composure and return to the courtroom. Taking a deep breath, I wiped my face, dried my eyes and re-entered the courtroom. Although I didn't know it at the time, my outburst had interrupted the proceedings significantly.

Motioning for me to approach the bench, the judge said, "The defense team is angry that you cried in the courtroom. By showing emotion in front of the jury, the defense contends you have tainted the jury and they are asking for a mistrial." Continuing, he said, "I did not notice any disturbance from you and I am going to deny their request for a mistrial."

Hearing this, I was deeply grateful. I certainly didn't want to go through another trial—that's for sure. No telling what I might discover about my mother. Fortunately, there wasn't one.

Closing arguments began the following morning. Otto's lawyer opened by saying, "Otto just happened to be in the wrong place at the wrong time." Other than that, his lawyer maintained that Otto was a great guy. He wasn't the villain the prosecution had painted him out to be. When the opposing counsel was finished trying to justify the unjustifiable, Girard went through every detail of the violent evening at Shamus' house. He walked them through my beating, torture and all the death threats. Essentially, Girard refuted everything Otto's lawyer had said. He made sure the jury knew that Otto was there of his own volition, for a purpose.

"You don't need to feel bad for Otto," the prosecutor told the jury. "We know Otto altered his schedule by calling in sick for work. He did this so he could be available at the crime scene to help Shamus." Continuing, Girard added, "Otto had many opportunities to back out, but he never did. He had the physical strength to stop Shamus, but he never did that either."

Proving they had conspired to commit the crime together, the prosecutor concluded his summation by theatrically running his finger across the throat. Addressing the jury at the same time, Girard said, "It's hard to imagine what Steven Sarkela went through in the closet that night. These criminals need to be brought to justice, and you, the jury, need to hold them accountable. You must convict Otto Z. Roddick for what he has done."

Once Girard concluded, the judge instructed the jury and handed over the case to them for deliberation. It was now in their hands and they retired to discuss the fate of Otto Roddick.

The following day, we were called and told to return to the courtroom immediately. Arriving shortly after 9 a.m., the room stirred as the jury entered, led by the foreman. Having finally reached a decision, they took their seats. The defense stood to face them while a guard blocked the door after allowing five tough-looking guys to sit down in the back of the courtroom. Curious, I looked at them. Their badges indicated they were U.S. Marshals.

A moment later, the jury foreman handed a piece of paper to the judge. Once he read it, he passed it to the court clerk to be read aloud. The tension in the room was palpable. As the verdict was being read, the marshals approached Otto from behind very slowly.

The clerk bellowed, "Count one, guilty. Count two, guilty."

Once the verdict was read, the judge ordered, "I will take Otto Z. Roddick into custody now."

With that, the U.S. Marshals closed in on Otto. Opening his jacket, one marshal prepared his stun gun while two others handcuffed Otto and led him out of the courtroom. Surprised by the swiftness of the officers, Otto never had a chance to use his karate skills on the marshals. Having seen him resist arrest once, the U.S. Marshals had no intention of having to subdue Otto again. Having been beaten by Otto, I understood why they took him into custody the way they did.

That's when I realized it was over—the entire mess. It was a surreal moment for me. I wasn't happy about it though. I just felt numb. Nevertheless, both Shamus and Otto had been convicted and I had been completely exonerated. It was a great victory, but I had also paid a terrible price to achieve it.

My wife understood this. Taking my hand, Lillemor led me out of the courthouse. Leaving the past behind, we were now free from Shamus' and Otto's malice. We got into our car and headed south—back to Florida to resume our new life together.

Life Moving Forward

t's been several years since the trial ended. Otto received a two year prison term and has now served his time. When he was released, he was deported to Belgium. I never saw him again and I don't expect to ever cross paths with him again. At least I hope I don't. Nevertheless, I remain hyper-vigilant, never going anywhere without my Glock.

I always keep my eyes open, rarely sleeping well. It's the continuous price I pay for nearly being murdered that night. My anxiety is not as debilitating as it used to be though, but it remains a problem. I suspect it will always cause me trouble. I'd like to think I will be completely free from it someday, but that might not happen. I wish it wasn't the case, but it is.

"Shamus is still in prison, serving a nine year sentence. As old and as ill as he is, few believe he will ever be a free man again. I hope they are right. I am forever thankful to God for saving me from that closet on that dark night.

As you can imagine, my relationship with my mother has never been resolved. As time passes, I doubt it ever will—but I remain hopeful. All I can do is hope for the best. After all, she will always be my mother. Jezzy has never been willing to be honest about what happened and I have never been willing to brush it aside like she asked me to a long time ago.

Every once in a while, Ahab tells someone that I stole condos from him while never mentioning his embezzlement or his involvement with Shamus and Otto. My dad was right about Ahab, wasn't he? I still miss my dad and think about him all the time.

I don't see much of my mother anymore after I have made many attempts to restore the relationship, asking for a confession of the truth concerning her involvement. I forgive her regardless, and that has freed me from the pain.

One person that has made forgiveness much easier has been Lillemor. Her love, support and consistent encouragement have been better than I could have ever imagined. I can't fathom how I would have survived without her. I make sure to tell her this everyday. I also make sure to tell her I love her everyday.

Things aren't always perfect between us. We have our moments, but they are few and far between. I'm a blessed man and I know it. My wife loves me and my relationships with my children have been restored. What more can a man ask for? All in all, I'd say my life is pretty good—and it's only getting better.

About the Authors

teven Sarkela was born in Battle Ground, Washington, a beautiful town near the Oregon border. One of eight children, he always wanted to make his way in the world. So, after graduating high school, Steven set off on his own and began his career in construction. He has worked in this industry for the past thirty years and has been quite successful at it.

Not content sitting on his laurels, Steven began a second business in marketing, which led to numerous speaking engagements on various topics. Loving construction and warm weather, he now builds luxury residential homes in South Florida. The father of five children, Steve enjoys spending his free time playing chess and jogging for exercise.

Having survived kidnapping and torture, Steve understand how difficult recovering from trauma can be. He wants to encourage those who have suffered from traumatic events and he wants to tell them that a new, richer life is possible.

Jack Watts, the father of five and grandfather of nine, lives in Atlanta, Georgia. A prolific author, Watts has written fourteen books, including his award-winning memoir, *Hi, My Name Is Jack*. He is also the author of the highly acclaimed Moon Series, *Unholy Seduction* and *Feet of Clay*.